APPLIQUÉ ART

Batsford

IN MEMORY OF MY DAUGHTER ZOE
WHOSE SHORT LIFE WAS THE INSPIRATION
FOR THIS WORK.

APPLIQUÉ ART

ORIGINAL IDEAS AND DESIGNS USING SIMPLE TECHNIQUES

STEWART MERRETT

B.T. BATSFORD LTD, LONDON

CONTENTS

INTRODUCTION

THE MEDIUM OF THREADS AND TEXTILES...EXPLODED AS A NEW AND EXCITING DIRECTION FOR MY FUTURE WORK AND LIFESTYLE.

Sometime in the middle of the seventies I fled to London from my home in Melbourne, Australia to recover and restore myself after a series of personal disasters including the shocking death of my little daughter Zoe. In London I stayed in the home of my life-long friend and artist Marion Appleton. This wonderful lady has always been a great source of inspiration and comfort to me and has spent much of her time collecting things of exquisite beauty such as books, objets d'art and many forms of antique textiles.

Desperate to find a new direction and purpose in my life I began to find a strong professional interest in these textile pieces that had contributed to Marion's wonderfully eccentric environment. My training as an illustrator and designer did not expose me to the medium of threads and textiles and now they exploded as a new and exciting direction for my future work and lifestyle. I realised that I could create lush and gorgeous images in this tactile and 'user-friendly' medium. I could create works that have an instant appeal and an 'ooh ahh!' response from the man and woman in the street. The 'ooh ahh!' level of response is very important to me as it indicates very quickly to a maker of imagery how well he or she is communicating with an audience. I was anxious to spend my time creating things of great beauty that had monumentality and not just 'smart arse' trendy pieces that could not stand the test of time — work that would demonstrate skill, craftsmanship and love as well as creativity. Soon I found myself plunging into a whole new world of textiles, both old and new. I had great fun teasing the sales people in London's famous auction rooms and rummaging through the stock of specialist shops all the time becoming more secure in my decision that I was on to a 'new' and wonderful idea.

I returned to Melbourne some time later, restored and resolved to begin the new phase of my life with textiles using their myriad textures in some form of colourful mosaic.

My first attempt at appliqué, after much procrastination, was of a fuchsia for some cushion covers. At the time I was frightfully proud of it but in retrospect I realise it was awful. Nevertheless it was a beginning. I had never really used a sewing machine before and soon realised that if I was to join all my textile mosaic pieces together I still had much to learn. An old industrial sewing machine purchased from a secondhand shop became my next challenge. Cushion covers were more than catered for by traditional craftspeople so the inspiration that appliqué could be 'bigger than Texas' had me projecting my drawings up to a huge scale and wondering if my machine and I could make these vast images materialise (ho! ho!).

After months of experimenting and a lot of fun they finally did. Aplekage (from appliqué and collage) was born and launched with my first one-man exhibition in the Melbourne suburb of Carlton. I invented the name Aplekage for my studio to draw attention to the centuries-old technique of appliqué used in a stunning and less traditional form. In the beginning I did not realise just how many applications this form of art could have: from the large public installations in hotels, casinos, office buildings, churches, and racecourses down to small domestic pieces, apparel, home wares and even architectural details such as cornices, walls and door panels. It is my hope that this book will enable others to appreciate the wonderful world of textiles and their applications. Hopefully it will inspire you too to 'have a go'.

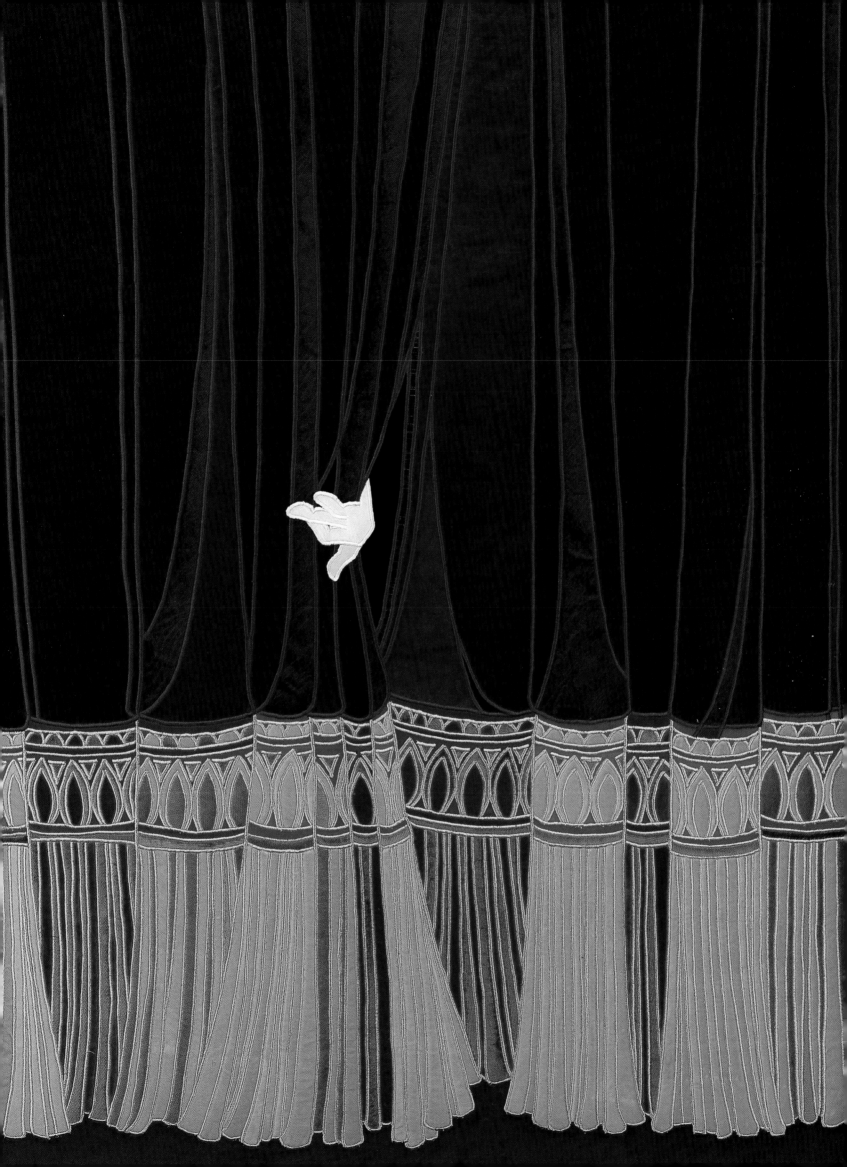

INSPIRATION

THE SKETCHPAD HAS BEEN OVERTAKEN BY THE CAMERA...TO HELP YOUR MIND SCAN THE INFINITE RANGE OF IMAGES.

The artist today has many new and highly technical processes with which to record images for their bank of inspiration and reference. I use my 35mm camera to record anything I think might provide an inspirational trigger for now or in the future. I believe the camera is an essential tool of trade for anyone working in the visual arts. The sketch pad has been overtaken by the camera in both quality and cost!

Understand how much more enjoyable one's task of creating iris and lily imagery is made with the use of these photographs. Here you have immediate reference for detail, structure, form and colour.

Your own style or technique may negate many of these initial elements in your final image but the ultimate success of it depends upon a thorough knowledge and understanding of your subject or source.

The inspiration for the appliqué Tissot and Mrs Newton, came from an early black and white photograph discovered in an old magazine.

aware of my fascination with the idea of masses of similar shapes and colours. I like the idea of lots and lots of the one thing. These red chillies are a simple and perfect inspirational source for many colours and tones of red that will impact the viewer's eye evoking strong taste and exotic aromas. This photograph could well be the catalyst for an image of a group of colourfully attired women in Guadeloupe with bundles of chillies piled high on their exotically swathed heads as they wend their way to the weekly market. Consider the textures you might use with this shiny and slippery fabrics or should you amuse yourself and confuse your viewer by making a piece of work in mad alternative cloths? Use the sight of these sensual aubergines and their unique colour contrasted against the gravid green beans to summon a contradictory image of a purple or black object such as the unfashionable reticule of some dowager princess discovered lying on a manicured croquet lawn. Similarly, the flowers of the lilies below, bring up any number of associations from trumpets to spot lights. Use photography to help your mind scan the infinite range of images.

These chillies seem to exude their latent strength — or is the mind pre-conditioned?

*Sensual aubergines are
perfect inspiration for
colour and form.*

*Are they trumpets?
Spotlights? Or merely a
group of beautiful
flowers.*

FRUIT

THE SIMPLE SENSUOUS SHAPES OF FRUIT APPEAR THROUGH HISTORY IN WORK OF EVERY KIND — FROM PINCUSHIONS TO PAINTINGS, FABRICS TO FANS, SILVER TO SARCOPHAGI, JEWELLERY TO JARDINIERES.

Simple, sumptuous and voluptuous shapes of fruit never cease to seduce artists to include them in their work. From furniture to frames, saddles to sculptures, light fittings to lecterns, pincushions to paintings, fabrics to fans, silver to sarcophagi, jewellery to jardinieres, and more — on the surface of any object that ever needed (and some that didn't) imagery, you will find fruit and flowers. They convey a feeling of well-being, beauty, peace and a sense of life's cycle.

Different fruit have been used as symbols in almost every culture in history. Indeed of all the decorative images ever used by artists and artisans, fruit and flowers stand alone! It is a delight to wander slowly through the produce markets of a city at the beginning of a working day and absorb the wonderful colour, life and shapes of the fruit and vegetables. Massed shapes and blocks of colour can restore even the most jaded soul and are an inspiration for any artist.

Fruit appear throughout my work in many different ways, from the abundant oranges of 'The Orange Vendor' to the uncomplicated symbolism of the pomegranate in the religious mural 'Heritage of Visions'.

My opportunity to idolise the images of fruit came with a commission to create an image for the foyer of yet another soulless office tower. My only source of inspiration was that the site on which the building stood had originally been a fruit and vegetable market (another historic jewel gone forever!).

'Framed Fruit and Vegetables' a mural of six large panels — carrots, peas, radishes, cherries, lemons and pears — now hangs as a gentle reference to the past.

Using the simple technique of colour choice this image of radishes could become beetroots, turnips or swedes — generating four works from one original drawing.

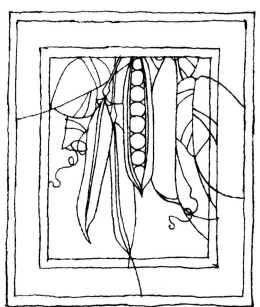

The three line drawings of radishes, peas and carrots are the vegetable images for the six panel mural of fruit and vegetables. The finished size of each of these panels is 1.25 metres wide, although my final drawings were no bigger than they appear here. If a drawing works well at this size I can be sure that it will be even stronger at large cartoon scale. I have learnt that it is a far less cumbersome process to create an image on a very small scale and then enlarge it to final size with an overhead projector than to draw the image directly as it will appear. This is a very personal way of working and may have something to do with my early training as a book illustrator rather than a muralist! However, I am able to make alterations and refinements very easily at postcard size whereas the same task at mural scale can take hours and hours.

In this series of framed images, I have extended some lines from the image out across the frame shapes. There are two reasons for doing this apart from the idea of integrating the frame with the subject. Breaking up the shapes in this way enables the use of more colour so that the finished piece emits a stronger feeling of textile intricacy. Secondly, smaller pieces of fabric are required and this reduces wastage of expensive, rare or well loved fabrics. Creating more shapes within

*Choice of contrasting or
complementary thread
colours can be crucial to
the success of the image.*

*Flip your image over and
create a mirror image
and a new work!*

the frame areas encourages the use of selected colours from the fruit and vegetable images to flow over and enhance the integration of the fruit and frame.

The image of 'Framed Pears' was the first in a large series work. These examples give a clear idea of how differently the same image can be treated by the choice of colour in fabric and thread. Even if the same fabric selection is decided for two or more works of the same image the appearance of each can be radically altered by the use of different coloured threads in the final satin stitching. A thread which contrasts dramatically with the chosen fabrics of a work will create a distinct mosaic appearance by isolating the shapes and colours. The use of blending tonal and complementary colours in the stitching thread will enrich the chosen fabrics and, in my view, enhance the work. Sometimes when it is impossible to make a final decision on thread colours it is worth considering the use of metallic threads such as gold and silver. These seem to work with any composition of colours and fabrics resulting in a luxurious finish.

I try to restrict my choice of threads so as not to interfere with the total image. The use of gold or silver thread across a whole work will assure you of stunning resolution. Metallic threads work well with all fabric because they reflect the colours they surround. The width of satin stitch will determine the density of colour and definition created. I steer a middle course and use a medium width stitch unless the image demands the stitching be a major attraction.

A contrasting thread colour around these plums would not have proved successful — the salmon pink thread spills across onto the frame and stands alone!

*The satin stitching of
the corrugated iron
background pieces is
an important element
in this image.*

The Prickly Pear, Indian Fig or Barbary Fig (*Opuntia ficus-indica*) was introduced to Australia from Central America in the 1930s as hedge rows for animal control on farms. It soon grew out of control and was declared a noxious weed. After forcing many families off their properties the Cactoblaster Moth was introduced to destroy the species and the infested countryside was eventually reclaimed. Occasional hedges of this grey-green cactus dotted with bright red fruit still remain. It was one of these I photographed on an excursion to a seaside resort. To add to the appeal of the image this row of stern and inpenetrable beauty stood against the side of a dilapidated corrugated iron shed.

I took a series of photographs in black and white of different sections of the hedge against its battered backdrop of silver-grey and rusted iron.

*The challenge was to
create a series of large
works from one small
hedge row of now
neglected prickly pear.*

(Top) One of my original black and white photographs of the prickly pear against the old tin shed.

(Above) This drawing was created by tracing my original photograph above and projected up to final cartoon size for immediate patterning and colour.

These photographs became my primary source for tracing and drawing the images. I believe it is better to work from black and white photographs and drawings. Invent the colour yourself. It is impossible to replicate the look of fabrics in paint, pencil or even colour photograph. Do not waste time preparing a coloured impression of what your finished work will never resemble. There are inherent dangers and frustrations in this approach. Work directly with a selection of possible fabrics as your palette. Spend time sifting through possible fabrics for their colours, textures and lightplay. Begin work directly once you have your palette of fabrics, discarding some fabrics and adding others as your brain begins to pick up creative momentum. I suggest it is worth restricting your choice of colours and fabrics. Make them work for you. Control is everything and it is easier with fewer ingredients than more — and the end result will be better. When I began work on this series of cactus images I discovered some embossed velvets and unusually marked satins in odd shades of grey greens and blues. I was puzzled by the possible commercial application of these fabrics. However they suited my purposes perfectly. It is unusual for me to incorporate patterned fabrics into my work. If an image demands a pattern then I create it with shapes of plain fabrics and threads (as in the 'Orange Vendor's Shawl' page 141). In the above panel I believe the inclusion of the patterned fabrics is a positive contribution to the appeal of the images.

The corrugated iron fence in the background of some of the works is not intended to feature but rather to enhance the Prickly Pear by supplying a very different texture and pattern as a foil to the flat bat-like leaves of this humble cactus.

The food writer Jane Grigson recommends that prickly pears peeled (very carefully), sliced, drenched in the juice of limes and sprinkled with the zest of limes make a truly refreshing dessert!

Completed panel of prickly pears created from the original source photograph opposite.

*Detail of the first
panel of 'Heritage for
Visions' illustrating
the pomegranate
flower bud.*

The sisters of the order of Saint John of God commissioned me to create a large mural for the foyer of their new hospital. It was important to develop imagery that was at once peaceful, decorative, beautiful and of comfort to many people in states of trauma. The mural is first seen when they arrive at the hospital and has to fulfil many different needs. I chose a very simple solution using the historically ornamental flower and fruit of the pomegranate imposed over a Celtic cross. The pomegranate is the symbol of Saint John of God and the origin of this caring order is an Irish one — hence the Celtic cross.

My concept was to illustrate the life cycle of the pomegranate from bud to flower: through fruit formation to final spectacular seed-burst against a background of the constant Celtic cross. The mural consists of five panels, each one-metre wide by two metres high. The title 'Heritage for Visions' was suggested by a marvellous woman, Sister Eugenia, who described this mural in the following way: 'the life cycle of the pomegranate illustrates the reality of each one's journey through life.' The wise nun may well be right. However, I will never cease to be amazed when I read and hear the opinions of others about the meaning of the work of artists. My research for botanical drawings of the pomegranate was assisted by the staff at the Royal Botanic Gardens of Kew in England. The surprisingly limited selection of drawings alerted them to the paucity of data available.

The Celtic cross is
constructed by the
random use of nap
direction of the Celtic
pattern velvet shapes.
This second panel depicts
the vivid flowering
of the pomegranate.

This tombstone was
reproduced in an old
issue of Country Life
magazine and supplied
the source for
the Celtic cross.

Greek mythology describes how Bacchus seduced a nymph with the promise of a crown. He then turned her into a pomegranate with its little crown-like calyx!

The pomegranate fruit begins to develop in the third panel of this contemplative mural.

The Saint John of God hospitals throughout the world are non-denominational. It was therefore important that the image of the cross was not paramount. By choosing only one velvet fabric with a good percentage of synthetic fibre so that it would respond dramatically to light, and by cutting the Celtic pattern shapes at random directions across the cloth the sculptural effect was achieved.

Each of the five crosses is the same but optically different as no two pieces of their Celtic patterns were cut from the velvet in exactly the same direction. This treatment of the cross allows the pomegranate to flourish and the viewers to make their own observations.

Saint John of God began health care work in the Spanish city of Granada, which has used the pomegranate as its crest since ancient times.

Carpet bags were once considered to be an integral part of everybody's clutter. Today there is a trend back towards reusable cloth carry bags in a desperate attempt to stop the world from choking to death on the ubiquitous plastic super market bag. Instead of buying or making a plain canvas bag with which to do your own marketing, perhaps I can encourage you to make your own simple carry bag out of more interesting fabrics. On to this bag you can appliqué an image or design and presto you have created something artistic that will always brighten your day.

I chose cherries for this bag of mine because I am enchanted by their clustered forms and luscious colours even though I know only too well that life is not a bowl of them! Fruit is not an imperative for a bag design, nor is it necessary to create something so complex.

Avoid making an image that travels to the edge of the bag as matching the sides can prove to be awkward. Alternatively only work one face of the bag and then you can make your design as intricate as you like. A simple sunface in bright yellows and golds on a blue denim bag would be stunning and quite easy to achieve. Zodiac signs or decorated initials for your friends and relatives are often a good starting point should you consider making a modern day carpet bag as a gift.

The dark background colour makes these cherries stand out strongly on the bag.

HOW TO DO IT

This simple, classic design is from a series of patterns which I prepared for my 'Framed Fruit' exhibition. Step by step instructions show you how to make your own appliqué.

Although the technique may appear to be fiddly, every step is essential to ensure your appliqué work is a success. Grasp the method and you will be able to proceed quickly; machine appliqué gives a faster result than traditional needlecraft.

Work with *two* copies of the design. One copy is pinned to a pin board (the placement pattern) while the other is cut up like jigsaw pieces. It is then attached with spray adhesive to the backs of appropriate fabrics, cut out and the coloured fabric pieces re-assembled on the placement pattern.

When the placement pattern is completely covered it is padded from behind and then adhered to the background fabric.

Misting with spray adhesive after every step is the secret of stability and accuracy and the complete sequence is fully illustrated in the following photographs.

The satin stitching clamps all the layers together and adds a distinctive outline. Leave the satin stitching until last on the foreground elements of the design. The order of work is — background first, foreground last.

As the sewing machine needle is hand guided, slight irregularities will inevitably occur and I regard them as an integral part of the technique. Puckers can throw shadows and highlights on fabrics and a wiggly line of stitching can often give new impetus to a design.

Enlarging the design

The pear design (my logo) can be made to any size you care to choose although here the basic pattern was enlarged to measure 35.5 x 45.5 cm (14 x 18 inches) which is two and a half times the size of the pattern diagram. Enlarge with a photocopier having first cut the pattern in half; you will need to do this as the finished design is larger than an A3 sheet of paper. Or you can trace the design onto a piece of tracing paper and, using the guidelines around the diagram, draw a grid over it of equally spaced lines. Back the tracing with a sheet of white paper so it is easy to read.

On paper large enough for the finished pattern and using set square and ruler, draw a grid of lines to the proportion of one square = 2.5 cm (1 inch). To transfer the pattern to this grid, mark the places on it which correspond to where the pattern lines intersect the pattern grid. Connect the markers using a ruler for straight lines and drawing the curves by hand. This master pattern can now be used for tracing two copies of the pattern onto stitch-and-tear, a non-woven non-stiff appliqué backing transparent enough for tracing.

Coding colours

Selecting fabrics and colours is always enjoyable and I often mix fibres and finishes, although here velvets in many colours and textures were chosen. After tracing two working copies of the pattern, assemble your range of fabric pieces and decide what will go where. Then cut out all the design shapes from the cutting pattern and position them on the placement pattern. If you prefer to work in a very orderly way you could colour code the cut pieces. Plastic headed pins in different colours were used here with lime-green leaves marked with light green pins, blue areas marked with white pins and so on. Put a pin into the corresponding fabric to remind yourself of the code. Or you can use letters and numbers to code colours and write them on your original enlarged pattern with the grid of lines, on a sticky label for the fabric and on the cut pattern pieces. There are six greens in the pear design on page 31 and they could be coded with the letter G from G1 to G6. Colour coding is a help when you re-position the fabric-faced pattern pieces on the placement pattern. However, sometimes it is fun to be less organised and sort it out as you go.

*Enlarge the pattern using
a photocopier or follow
the instructions to
enlarge using the grid
lines marked.*

YOUR STEP-BY-STEP GUIDE TO MACHINE APPLIQUÉ

MATERIALS
Stitch-and-tear (lightweight non-woven backing); Spray adhesive; Selection of fabric scraps; Fabric for backing; Dacron batting; Plastic headed pins, multi-coloured; Selection of machine threads.

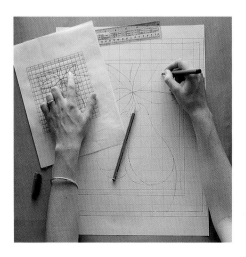

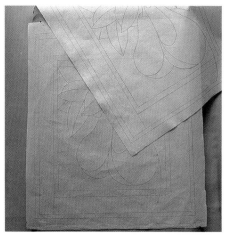

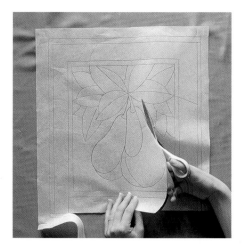

1. Following instructions on page 30, enlarge the pattern to the required size.

2. From the enlarged pattern, trace two copies onto two separate pieces of stitch-and-tear and pin one to a pinboard.

3. Cut out all the design elements from the other traced pattern.

4. Using the pins or the alternative method in *Coding colours*, position and code cut pieces on placement pattern.

5. In a well ventilated room, spray the pinned-on pieces with adhesive a few at a time.

6. Take pattern piece and place sticky side down, on *back* of appropriate fabric. Press firmly with warm iron.

7. Cut out the pattern piece which is now faced with fabric. Treat all pattern pieces in this way.

8. Mist the placement pattern with spray adhesive prior to re-positioning the cut patterns with fabric attached.

9. Re-position the fabric-faced pattern pieces on the placement pattern.

10. Cut a piece of Dacron batting the same size as the pattern and spray it on one side with adhesive.

11. With your hands, firmly press the wrong side of the work onto the sticky side of the Dacron batting.

12. Trim to the perimeter of the design.

13. Turn the assembly over and spray the back of the Dacron with adhesive.

14. Turn it back to the right side and press the assembly onto the background fabric.

15. Satin stitch through all layers following instructions for the order of work on page 30.

FLOWERS

I HAVE ALWAYS FOUND GREAT PERSONAL JOY IN THE INFINITE
BEAUTY OF FLOWERS — EVEN DURING MY DARKEST AND MOST
IMPOVERISHED PERIODS I HAVE RECEIVED GREAT SOLACE
JUST FROM THE SIGHT OF A FEW BLOOMS.

I am only one of legions of people in the arts and crafts world who, since life began, have used the form and colour of flowers as an inspiration for much of their work.

Massed flowers in markets, fields or vase are my ultimate delight — to come upon a field of brilliantly coloured wild flowers while driving through the countryside is even more entrancing for me than a planned visit to the acreages of the world's most spectacular bulb and perennial flower growers, or even a tour of the famous Chelsea Flower Show! Just to stand among these vivid natural carpets of colour and perfume restores my belief in the continuation of the planet.

The singular spectacle of an unexpected orchid cascading down from a tall rainforest palm is an exciting statement of life on earth. The sight of the first crocus after a long, cold, grey winter clearly announces an end to misery and introspection and the beginning of a new warmth, encouragement and hope. The purity and clarity of these images and millions more are a challenge for any artist or poet. I sometimes wonder if mankind's attempts to record such exquisite beauty tread presumptuously in the realm of the unknown.

Flowers have played their role throughout our history as symbols or decorations at celebrations and ceremonies — sometimes they are used as national emblems or on currency and postage stamps.

The iris is one of the oldest cultivated plants in history. Its luminescent colours and elegant forms dare every artist to use it in their work. Illustrations of this exquisite flower and its leaves decorate the walls of the botanical chamber in the temple of Thutmoses I beside the Nile at Karnak.

The Egyptians considered the iris to be a symbol of eloquence using its shape, colour and form throughout their decorative arts.

In the 12th Century AD the iris was immortalised when it was used as the inspiration for that now classic symbol the fleur-de-lis, emblem of the French royal family.

The Dutch and Italian old masters preferred to include this fragile flower in their art as a symbol of the divinity of Christ.

Irises later figured in the organic designs of the art nouveau period

The folding screen is both a very practical piece of furniture and also the ultimate device for bringing decoration into the living space. The Chinese and Japanese have known this for centuries and modern day artists such as David Hockney continue to use this medium.

These irises were my first attempt at a folding screen. Each panel is approximately 750mm wide by two metres tall and they were originally created for my own house. However it has since found its way into the beautiful living room of a home in Western Australia.

The man-eating scale of my Irises may be overwhelming for some but I was anxious to demonstrate the link between the colours and textures of the delicate petals and beards with those of satins, silks and velvets.

When buying the satins for this work I was confronted with so many magnificent hues of purple, lilac and blue that I felt I had to include every one of them in this work. Discipline, however, is everything when it comes to creating something of intrinsic value and I soon learnt that 'less is more'. I restricted

my palette to a few of my favourite shades and a couple of what I call 'odd' colours to use as a foil against the major colours.

   This image could be made time and time again, if you had the strength and patience, in any colourway at all. Iris grow in such a multitude of colours and shades that even if you are a stickler for detail the possibilities are seemingly endless.

   The leaves of this iris image are of equal importance to me as the flower. Without these stunning grey green spearlike shapes the

colour and shape of the flower would not succeed. Nature knows more about balance than the world's greatest designers and the iris is one flower whose bloom does not stand alone successfully. I chose a selection of different grey green fabrics for the varying texture and colour of the stems giving the area depth and interest. The background colour onto which the entire image is worked is a carefully chosen 'nothing green' velvet. I did not want to challenge the iris image — only just to quietly complement it.

Different grey green fabrics provide texture and colour for the iris stems and act as a foil for the brilliant flowers.

A panel of Strelitzia reginae *is almost two metres in length and proved to be very popular with the exotic flower heads and big bladed leaves.*

The strelitzia comes from a strange and rather dramatic family of perennials closely related to the banana family. In its native South Africa it is known as the crane flower because of its resemblance to the head of that exotic tropical bird.

During the 1970s this flower became the status symbol of style. It was considered to be fearfully chic to arrange one of these superb specimens in a simple vase and announce your awareness of the purest sense of design! Images of this flower appeared on everything from cushion covers to porcelain.

The temptation to express these forms in appliqué was inevitable. The joy of clashing bright orange silks and velvets against vivid blue and dusty green was controlled by the choice of bronze green shot taffeta for the boat-like spathes from which these colours burst. Old green curtain pieces and an unusual slubbed fabric feature largely in the construction of the leaves and stalks against a background of grey-green velvet.

All the colour in this image is concentrated in the man eating sized flowers while the leaves and stalks form a quiet tropical accompaniment.

The leaves, although clearly geranium, have been made to appear huge and tropical.

Little is known about the origins of the humble geranium. One legend has Mohammed hanging his shirt out to dry over a mallow plant which then magically turned into a geranium.

In Victorian times geraniums were the flower of the very poor, which they attached to the walls of their houses or used as a splash of colour on a window ledge. These days this look is regarded as stylish simplicity.

The exciting part of constructing this work was the opportunity to use different white fabrics in the making of the flower heads, with the dense orange eye as the only bright colour.

*Different colourways for
the same image make
choices difficult.*

Cyclamen I, II and III illustrate a well documented problem for many artists. You succeed in creating a black and white image which you deem to be very successful and then agonise over a colour interpretation.

These three favourite pieces are an example of this creative crisis and process. I enjoyed creating three variations of the one image but still had difficulty restricting myself to only three colour interpretations.

Fortunately the connoisseur who purchased them appreciated each of my colour schemes and bought the lot!

These cyclamen were the first 'framed' images that I created, there have been many others since.

The pink petals of this bloom may well be unique.

The waterlily is the flower of purity and resurrection. Every year it rises, pure and virginal, from the murky depths below the surface — a living symbol of life starting anew.

From the rainforests of the Amazon basin to the wetlands of Kakadu in northern Australia; from the reflection pools of mystical Indian temples to the mannered garden ponds of 16th Century Italian villas — the waterlily floats serenely on the surface of water all over the world.

The ancient Egyptian civilisation idealised the waterlily, which they called the Lotus of the Nile. The shapes and representation of this simple flower became an integral part of their culture; it was used to decorate everything from architecture and furniture to jewellery and clothing. Many modern symbols in common use can be traced back to the simple shapes of the lotus or waterlily.

Claude Monet suffered artistic torment in his love affair with the waterlilies which floated on the lake at Giverney. His need to keep painting these blooms in every light and configuration consumed years of his life and produced a vast collection of exquisite waterlily imagery that remains as one of his gifts to humanity.

Waterlilies have been a favourite subject in my work for a long time, I have produced a number of appliqué works using them alone or as part of other images. The use of these elegant blooms with black swans (page 82) demonstrates one more fanciful application.

This panel is waterlilies pure and simple. It is two metres long. The flowers are neither strictly waterlily nor lotus but a blend of both to suit the desired effect of this very simple and restful image. The simple shapes of

Each year the waterlily rises pure and virginal from the murky depths.

the flowers and the pads made this piece very easy to construct. The diminishing sizes of the pads give the illusion of perspective to the horizon with just a spark of things to come in the arrival of a lone bud about to burst!

The flowers in this piece have all been made from different shades of white through to deep pink with centres of pale yellow vel-vets and satins.

The two background velvets used in this work can be the same. Simply run the cloth in opposite directions for the sky and the water and join them at the horizon before putting the rest of the work into place for stitching. This trick gives the impression of two completely different colours, the light works its magic with the opposite directions of the velvet's nap. Using one colour of heavily napped velvet in many different directions in a work can often create a very subtle and effective result, an example of this is the Celtic cross in my pomegranate panels on page 25.

The diminishing sizes of the pads give the illusion of perspective.

The inspiration for so many of Monet's paintings.

Three topiary rose panels commissioned for a private dining room.

The rose is so involved in myth and legend its origin has been completely obscured. This wonderful flower has been the symbol of love, secrecy, martyrdom, virginity, youth and the badge of kings and countries. To this day it survives as a gentle expression and symbol of love from one person to another. The Empress Josephine of France commissioned one of the most notable collections of rose images during the late eighteenth and early nineteenth century. Josephine's extraordinarily comprehensive garden of roses at Malmaison was painted by the brilliant watercolour artist Pierre Joseph Redouté. The final work consisted of one hundred and sixty eight varieties comprising three volumes entitled *Les Roses*. There are many varieties of the rose growing all around the world. Some are large and blowzy for old ladies hats and some are tiny and tight to decorate a wedding cake. Some creep, others climb, some grow as shrubs while others can be huge unruly bushes. The double or single blooms come in amazing shades of red, pink, orange, yellow, cream, white and lavender. I cannot imagine why some scientists today believe we need to develop a blue rose!

I have always admired the Tenniel illustrations for Lewis Carroll's *Alice in Wonderland*. When I was commissioned to create three vertical panels for a sumptuous dining room I grasped the opportunity to develop my own interpretation of the topiary roses that the dreaded Queen of Hearts had redecorated to match her suit.

These three tall works are alternated with mirror panels along a wall. The soft colours of the flowers and leaves are set against a 'brown paper' colour velvet background to complement the existing colours of the room. These very intricate designs are made up of many similar shapes. This called for a lot of patience from both me and my assistant Barbara in putting all the pieces together. This task was made more pleasurable by the two metre height of the trees and the feeling that one might well have been working under orders from the Queen of Hearts herself!

The Scottish artist and architect Charles Rennie Mackintosh was a subtle influence on this particular work. I find his watercolour and ink painting of flowers a great inspiration. His sense of colour, design and style with abstract shapes and natural forms demonstrate great graphic sensibility and originality.

Many of the similar shapes which make up the roses appear different by the simple use of changing colours. Two of the panels are a mirror image of each other while the centre panel stands alone. I used this balanced approach to give a feeling of formality to the work. The whole project was stitched in subtle tonings of the colours of the image — pale pink for the roses, pale green for the leaves and lilac grey for the branches and the trunks. The second edition of these images was appliquéd onto a very pale green velvet background and stitched in gold and silver metallic giving the finished works a totally different quality.

One of the most awkward problems with an image as large and intricate as the Topiary Roses is to retain all the completed jigsaw in place for the duration of the sewing process.

One of the few vivid memories from early childhood is the centres of the white daisies which grew in the Victorian flower beds of my grandparents garden. Ever since I have been intrigued by their extraordinary black-purple velvet colour. Thirty five years later when a friend gave me an exquisite silk velvet in this colour I had no alternative but to create a work celebrating the white daisies. Simply called 'Daisies' this graphic image is the first of many works where I played with the 'still-life' tricks of window, wall, door and tabletop as props for my primary subject and passion — flowers.

'Daisies' began as a very quick thumbnail sketch about the size of a matchbox which was then enlarged, without any further refinement, to over a metre high. Simplicity and boldness result from this technique which creates a fresh and lively image. Sometimes I am driven to refine my imagery because I have lost faith in my original drawing but the reality is usually that the very first idea and drawing is the best for all the primary reasons of honesty, simplicity and directness.

Daisies from a childhood memory make up this bold image.

The heady perfume of lilies in the house was once believed to envelope the occupants in holiness and protect them from witchcraft and evil!

The arum lily panel was the first piece of appliqué I ever sold and it would be hard to discover a simpler flower. This supremely elegant member of the callas family has a history almost as turbulent as the diva who shares the name. Always a flower of celebration, through the centuries many cultures adopted it as a symbol for death and used it only for funeral biers and wreaths. Isadora Duncan scandalised the public of her day by doing naughty dances with a wreath of arum lilies around her head which nevertheless helped demystify it s unfair connotation of the grim reaper.

The simplicity of the white fold swathed around a clear yellow stamen topping a thick translucent stem of pure pale green, makes this stylish specimen an obvious target for many applications in the world of arts. Though this elegant plant is often still relegated to railway cuttings and rarely visited areas of a garden, sensitive interpretations like those by the great photographer Robert Mapplethorpe have helped people to appreciate it as the elegant flower it always was.

The original concept for this luxurious restaurant mural began long before it was ever commissioned. While spending an overcast weekend away at a seaside town I wandered off from the group of friends to photograph things of interest. Suddenly I came upon a small group of arum lilies flowering their hearts out in a nearby swamp.

The black and white photographs of these plants sat in my file for some time before I was commissioned to execute a 'Rousseau-like' mural in appliqué for a restaurant in a casino in Darwin, at the tropical top end of Australia.

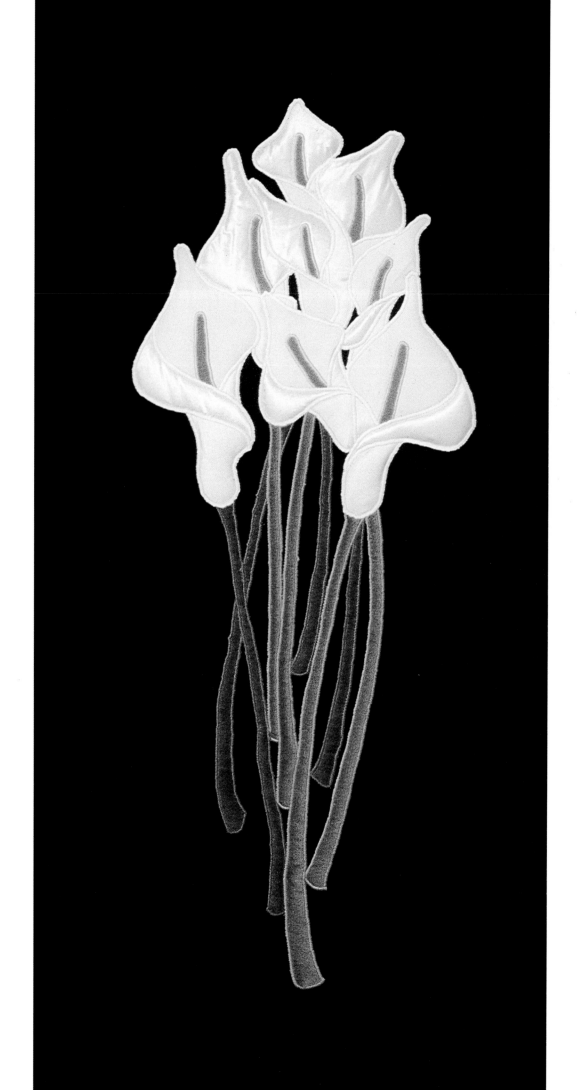

There is a belief that
when Eve fled the
Garden of Eden in
hysterics her tears could
be traced by the lilies that
grew from where her
salty droplets had
splashed the ground!

The client had already decided on the colours for this beautifully appointed room so I worked the image onto the same cloth as that used to upholster the long banquette thereby making the mural appear to be completely integrated.

Intricacy and detail were achieved by the use of assorted green fabrics and shapes in the construction of the bank of lily leaves.

A subtle choice of green stitching was used to blend the leaf shapes (unlike the contrasting effect used in 'White Geraniums', page 41) so as not to break up the overall effect of dense foliage but still ensure interest.

It is important in commissions of this nature to create a work of great beauty and interest but not one that will so overwhelm a room that patrons are made to feel precious about it or themselves.

The *Lilium* is my favourite flower. To the most interesting of my photographs I combined the best areas of each into my initial drawing. This drawing was then divided in half vertically to form two narrow panels. I then made a mirror image of each of these and alternated the panels along the great length of the wall.

A repeating pattern such as this gives a frieze effect and enhances the formality of the architecture. The lily shoots up with authority in early spring growing to a tall and strong green spear of stem with leaves and large pendulous buds. The flowers of the lily are breathtakingly beautiful in their waxy trumpet like simplicity. Their enchanting scent is so intense that many find it overwhelming. Once the fabulous act is complete the lily dies away to prepare itself for a repeat performance next year.

The ancient Greeks used lilies to make wine and cooking oil — 'first take 1000 lilies…'

The Madonna lily was brought to England by the Romans where it soon became the symbol of the Virgin and became enmeshed in Christian visual arts ever after.

However we know this beautiful bloom existed long before the Romans as its image has been discovered on Cretan vases and other decorative objects from the Minoan period 3000-1100 BC. It is thought to have been a symbol of fertility during this period unlike The Middle Ages when monks used a poultice of lily roots for the treatment of boils.

I do not believe in being slavishly botanical about my images — it is important that the idea of the image is communicated very clearly and easily. Botanical details can sometimes surprise and confuse the viewer and often impose design demands that are quite unnecessary. Take from your subject only the

shapes and details that please you and improve the work you have conceived. Try not to become too bogged down in esoteric detail and edit out anything that does not enhance your 'big picture'. This lilium screen is once again, basically a study in green and white. There are many other colours of liliums but I do seem to have an obsession with white flowers! I believe they have a very tranquil quality and are most appropriate for use on a piece of furniture.

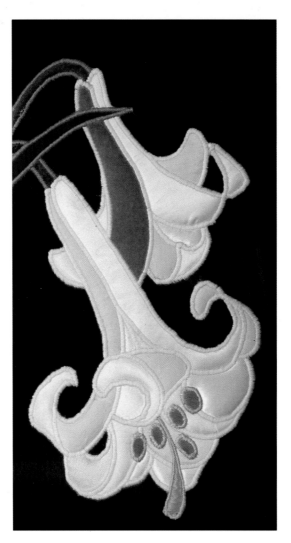

The background velvet onto which these lilies are worked was an exciting discovery in a discount store. It is an impossible colour to describe as it changes from a dark antique green to a greeny gold brass colour depending on the light source and the time of day. Although the leaves and stalks of the lilies are made of velvets they remain fairly static in their colour as they are comparatively small pieces and so allow for substantial play of light. The background with its large empty areas of velvet changes dramatically around the lily images from night to day.

This lilium screen is an interpretation of the classic lily — a simple image of the purest features.

The very common name of this most exotic plant is strap cactus. It is, of course, an *Epiphyllum* which is vaguely connected to its cactus cousins and never referred to as one by those who know about such matters. This beautiful specimen growing in a pot was given to me by an enthusiastic plant woman named Elizabeth Taylor — hence the title of this work 'Elizabeth Taylor's Gift' — and caused much gossip when it was displayed in public. Many of the social set of gallery goers could not fathom my connection with such a megastar. Could there be more than one person with such a name? Soon after accepting this thoughtful gift I made a drawing of it during its very brief blooming period. From this initial drawing the first work nearly two metres in length was made. This *Epiphyllum* with its luxurious flower heads and unusual leaf formation made a perfect subject for my appliqué art.

I was able to use a wonderful assortment of reds, deep pinks, burgundies and magentas in the flowers and a very diverse selection of fabrics from tweeds to satins in the different greens for the fleshy leaves. The padding behind the leaves, buds and flowers accentuates the form and the different textures of each.

Notice how less than one third of the total surface area of this panel is actually appliquéd — the placement and design of the image are crucial to its success. It is not necessary to applique every square centimetre of space in a work. The empty areas of any work can be just as important as the image itself. 'Elizabeth Taylor's Gift II' is a section taken from my original drawing for the first work, enlarged and worked on a panel over 1.5 metres tall. This piece enabled me to accentuate the exotic blooms of this plant even more by incorporating only two of its flowers and masses of empty background.

The padding behind leaves and buds accentuates the form and different textures.

Intriguing colour changes occur to the stems, mirror, wall and table cloth as they appear through the water in the vase. Imagine the fun you could have with a goldfish bowl! 'Daffs' is one of the collection of cut flower images to which 'Daisies' (p 49) belongs. My intent with these very simple images was to illustrate the beauty of cut flowers — to isolate them without any other clutter or objects often thought necessary for a still-life. This elegant work utilises the simplest vase possible combined with a very plain mirror frame and tabletop. All emphasis is on the flowers and buds with particular attention given to the stems of the daffodils and the colour changes above and below the waterline. The idea of the water is only perceived by the use of these colour changes. I have not bothered with the business of reflections in the glass vase (how do we know it's glass?). They would only break up the clean shapes of the image and complicate the message. This is a study in green and yellow and was the first 'Daffs' piece to be made. The second piece (opposite page) is even more restricted in colour than the first. Once again I return to my obsession with greens and whites with just the smallest touch of bright colour to make the whites whiter. I have studiously avoided any reference to the God Narcissus after whom these trumpets of spring are named and chosen not to see any reflections in the mirror that might detract from the elegance of the work.

'Daffs' is a study in green and yellow. All emphasis is on the flowers and buds.

Australia's reputation for unique flora and fauna has belatedly spread world wide. Tourists travel days to visit and experience these natural wonders, to feast their eyes on the thousands of acres of nature's amazing spring and summer carpets. Only in recent years have these stunning blooms been farmed commercially and sent off to the flower markets of the world. When I was first invited to create a range of appliqué designs for sale as do-it-yourself kits it seemed appropriate to make a collection based on wildflowers from Australia. Like most countries and states Australia uses its indigenous varieties for various floral symbols. I chose to use these symbolic blooms as the basis for this collection. The

bright yellow wattle which garlands the Australian bushland in the middle of winter is the symbol of the nation. Usually expressed in the harshest yellows and greens on sports apparel I preferred to interpret the wattle by using softer blue-greens and gentle pale chromes and would encourage you to do the same. The flowering eucalyptus or gum, as it is commonly known, is the floral emblem of Australia's best kept secret — the island state of Tasmania. The variety chosen for official purposes is white flowering but eucalypts bloom in all shades from white through to a very dark crimson. A very fine and complicated bloom the flowering gum is considered by some to be a more appropriate subject for embroidery of

ladies' hats and skirts, but with simplification it works quite well for appliqué. The floral emblem of New South Wales is the fabulous waratah. This dramatic bloom takes its name from the Aboriginal word 'waratah', which means flame or torch. If you ever have an opportunity to view this great flower in its natural habitat you will quickly understand this connection. The flower allows for a real indulgence in the thousands of shades and textures of red.

The largest state of Australia uses the most exotic of this collection as its own — the Kangaroo Paw — named very obviously because of its similarity to the paws of Australia's most well-known animal symbol. This rush-like plant has many different varieties and flowers in various colour combinations. Red and green, like Christmas, seem the most traditional. The English sailor who discovered Australia had a small town named after him, Cooktown, the place where he first landed in the tropical state of Queensland. This state has since adopted a bright pink rainforest orchid also named Cooktown, as its floral symbol. The Pink Heath is the most European in appearance of this collection and is the symbol of my home state of Victoria. My Pink Heath resembles more an English foxglove than the rather insipid native plant. I suppose one failure in a group of seven is not a bad average.

The seventh and final design in my collection of Australian floral emblems is the Sturt Desert Pea. This spectacular plant is the symbol of the state of South Australia, the majority of which is desert. An early explorer called Sturt who had lots to do with exploring and opening up the hinterland rode off into the desert with his party since when many stories and myths about their adventures and Mr Sturt's death have been passed on. One of these stories tells about the connection between the birth of this plant and the red of the explorers blood spilt on the desert sands. However I suspect this European fable bears no relevance to the Australian aboriginals' dreaming of this vibrant pea flower. Clearly the colours and the weird shapes of this dense ground cover have been an obvious choice for Australian artists who have used its image on everything from ceramics to furniture and even pressed tin ceilings.

It seemed appropriate to use the floral emblem of the state of South Australia when I was commissioned to make a large floor to ceiling foyer mural for the Adelaide headquarters of an international advertising agency.

The image for this work is exactly the same as the small cushion size of my kit design (opposite page). I have only extended the image by repeating the flowers through the centre of the mural to correct the proportions to the wall. When the flower and leaf shapes are enlarged to this size they virtually become abstract shapes and the people using the space enjoy sections of the image rather than viewing the whole mural. Coincidentally the corporate colours of this company were red and black so I was able to accommodate the wishes of everyone from the chairman of the board to the smiling receptionist for whom this work was her daily environment. Most of the fabrics used in this very large piece are the same as those used in the much smaller image opposite with the exception of the black eyes. There I incorporated some black patent leather in the hope of generating some deviant behaviour in what was an otherwise very conservative atmosphere.

PROJECT

FLORAL INITIALS

First decide who is to be the recipient of your largesse and then, using the first letter of their name, make up a luxurious appliquéd cushion. Take a flower with the same initial and use this to entwine the letter in an interesting way. Allow parts of the letter to disappear behind the flowers and foliage leaving just enough of it exposed to ensure legibility. This is not an original idea, illuminated letters have been used for centuries by monks and scribes to decorate their books. I have chosen to decorate this letter with a personal favour-ite — the Hippeastrum. This simple flowering bulb blooms in a number of different colours and its very broad petals and leaves are perfect for using contrasting textures.

Select silks and satins for the flower heads and velvets for the leaves and stalk. Notice the choice of threads used in this piece and how I have defined the letter with metal-lic silver thread to enhance its legibility. A limited use of colours in the satin stitching helps to harmonise the disparate fabric tex-tures and colours in any work.

Note:

The background of this alphabet panel is cut on the cross so the pile of the velvet catches the light and produces a rich sage green. Although this takes more fabric than would be required were the background cut on the straight, there is never waste with appliqué; offcuts are a rich resource of colour and texture for future projects.

You will need:

Sufficient stitch-and-tear (lightweight non-woven backing) for two full size patterns; Spray adhesive; Selection of fabric scraps; Fabric for backing 80cm (32 inches) square; Dacron batting; Plastic headed pins, multi-coloured; Selection of machine threads; Particleboard 60 x 60cm (24 x 24 inches); Heavy duty stapling gun.

Directions:

For the letter to be 40cm (16 inches) square, enlarge the pattern using the grid system as explained on page 30 with 1 square = 3cm (1 and a quarter inches).

Read the *How To Do It* chapter on page 29 and cut out and assemble the appliqué according to the basic instructions and step-by-step guide. Be generous with the mistings of spray adhesive so that the assembly is well secured before you start using the sewing machine.

Remember that the background fabric is cut on the cross. Make the border section smaller or larger if desired; the panel photographed has a 12cm (almost 5 inch) border.

When stitching, complete the background sections before doing the foreground.

To stretch the appliqué, locate the centre of the assembly and the centre of the particleboard and attach the fabric to the board at this point with a drawing pin. Ensuring that the centres stay in line, pull the excess fabric of one side around to the back of the board and staple at the centre. Then work on the opposite side, stretching the fabric around to the back and securing with a staple. Repeat with other two sides keeping work taut and checking that the appliqué is properly centred. If it has slipped out of alignment, remove staples and start again.

When the centres on all sides are satisfactorily stapled, work gradually out to the corners, stapling on opposite sides as before. On the corners, fold fabric in pleats.

Insert a screw eye on each side of panel's back and thread with picture-hanging wire.

The ultimate in graphic design and camouflage, the vulnerability of the species is underlined by this family's sentinel.

ANIMALS

NATURE IS EVER CHANGING. ENVIRONMENT AND THE INSTINCT FOR SURVIVAL HAVE CONSPIRED TO DEVELOP STUNNING VARIATIONS IN THE WILD ANIMALS OF OUR PLANET.

Every day the numbers and spread of our animals are reduced while our attempts to protect them are puny. No one, especially an artist, can ignore the animal kingdom. I believe it is the responsibility of artists everywhere to evoke as much imagery as possible to remind people how endangered the world's magnificent animals have become. One cannot help but be impressed by the ingenious range of camouflage and protective skills and devices developed by so many of our wild animals. The zebra or the leopard have only to be mentioned and everybody knows immediately what colours, patterns or shapes are involved. These survival tricks were adopted centuries ago for use as classic patterns and decoration in all the visual arts.

Animals can reveal themselves in the white on white landscape of the polar bear to the red and terra cotta plains of the Serengeti where the lion reigns supreme. Or there is the lush tropical green rainforest home of the orang utan in Borneo.

Colours and creatures, environments large and small, herds, prides or solo voyagers, fables and facts, friend or foe, nasty and nice — think of any mood, legend, or personal fantasy and there is a selection of unique animals from which to choose imagery. The ultimate in graphic design and camouflage — the zebra, is a natural source of inspiration for artists. Obviously this piece is a study in black and white with a splash of highlight colour on the nose of a solitary face. I used a number of different whites and creams with blacks and browns to create this image but their subtlety is barely visible from the printed page.

Only martians could use
this scarcely visible
make-up mirror with
any success!

The threatened orang utans of Borneo were the spark for this unusual mirror panel. The height of the finished work is 1.25 metres and it's proportions suit a smaller domestic space. This was my first work incorporating a mirror and the free hanging semi-dimensional applique used on the animal's arm and hands. I chose a green mirror — possibly unwisely — so as not to create too strong a circular shape that could overwhelm the image. On this occasion I could not afford my usual cavalier approach to sewing the back as the reverse of the orang utan's arms and hands are reflected in the mirror for any fine seamstress to scrutinize. Some of the fabrics in this animal were purchased from secondhand clothing shops. My original intention on moving into applique was to use only re-cycled fabrics but, like any good baby boomer, I grew bored with faded, smelly, garments, curtains and bedspreads of the past and turned to the fabric supermarkets of today where everything is made easy and expensive.

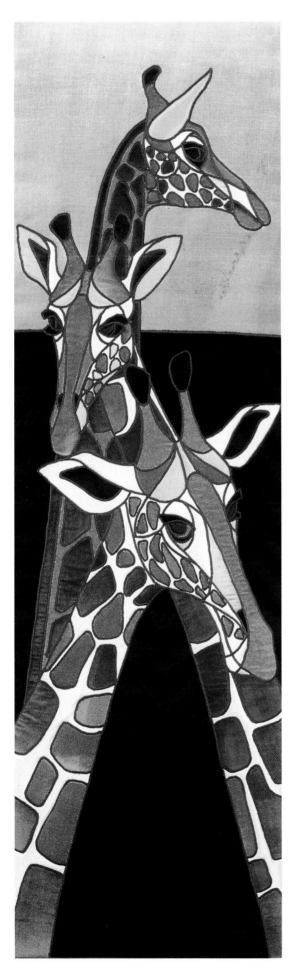

The giraffe is an image from childhood associations with Noah's Ark, Doctor Dolittle, and other stories. Of all the African animals the giraffe is the most visually extraordinary and therefore the most easily recalled. I remember this work as the first animal image I ever made in appliqué. I wanted to reproduce the wonderful dappled pattern of their prehistoric necks and feature the doe-like appeal of their gentle faces. These animals are a fantastic combination of the weirdest shapes and beautiful details and really demand a collection of images to celebrate properly their unique place on our planet. Imagine how different this image would appear if I had not made the background into two shapes by including a horizon line. Apart from creating an illusion of depth this very simple device allows for another big block of strong colour to focus around the furthest giraffe's head.

Mud, mud, glorious mud! These lugubrious animals adore it. Their great sculptural forms half submerged along the banks of the Limpopo river confirm it. Not until the hippopotami eventually move can you be certain they are not merely enormous boulders strewn along this legendary African waterway. The sight of the massive shapes of slow-moving giants coincided with the arrival of some mottled and flawed velvet which was bought in a job lot of fabrics. The opportunity to express their sculptural form in a fabric that echoed the leathery brown and pink skin of the hippopotamus was too good to miss. I created an image of huge hippo bums half submerged and contrasted the large trapunto shapes with the detail and character of their heads and faces, paying particular attention to their very quirky ear configuration.

The horizon, once again, gives the illusion of a depth of field while presenting the technical advantage of using one length of uncut cloth. The placid faces of these 'hippos' are the only detail in this work.

Circles often appear in my images representing moons or suns. In this possum screen the pale moon lends a Japanese quality to this art form. It is also a clear reference to the nocturnal nature of the exquisite possum poised atop the banksia bloom. This image is very spidery in configuration and required much control during the sewing so that when the work was finally stretched, all the background shapes between leaves, cones and flowers came clean and free of ruches and wrinkles. I believe it is better if the difficult process of appliqué is not in evidence when a work is complete. It is not the role of the viewer to suffer for their art! This sweet screen stands 1.5 metres tall and is my favourite work of Australiana to date. It was purchased so swiftly from an exhibition that I have no knowledge as to its current whereabouts.

This image relies upon the horizon line to define the extent of the river mud in which the 'hippos' are lying.

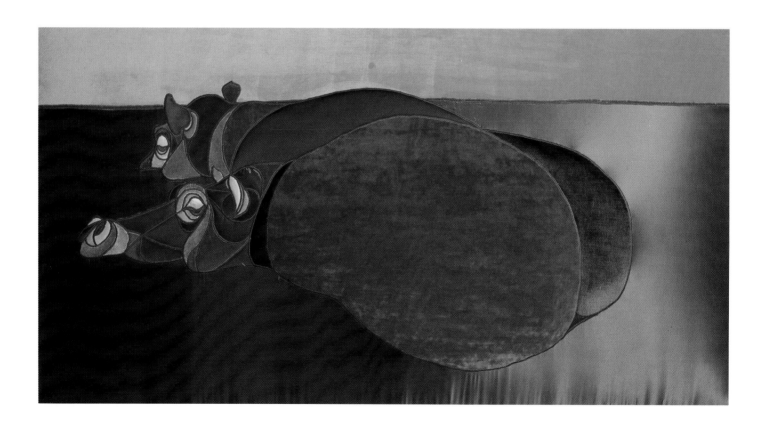

The major component of this image is the environment but the tiny possum is its focal point.

The 'Great Grey Elephant' uses less theatrics and is softer and more contemplative than its predecessor.

I purposely made one eye a different colour from the other not just for artistic reasons of light and shade but also to give viewers the opportunity to ask me if I was aware of my mistake. It's good to keep them talking!

The genesis of a commission is often amazing. This stately 'Golden Elephant' was commissioned in Australia as a seventieth birthday gift for a man in the Hague who has an insatiable fetish for elephants. He surrounds himself with elephantasia of all description and now he has a very large elephant appliqué too! I purposely chose to treat this stately member of the animal kingdom as an icon by surrounding the work with an intricate frame and decorating the subject with a very lavish head-dress and trunk ornaments. It was, after all, a celebration of the biggest land animal *and* a seventieth birthday!

One could easily assume that the image of 'Rams' was developed by this Australian artist to promote what was once my country's primary export — wool. These are Merinos and formerly were a symbol of our nation's wealth. The world has changed and natural fibres are no longer in the same demand and cannot compete with synthetic alternatives. Rams was a very corny solution to a common problem of finding an idea for an image.

I was invited to create a work for a charming family to hang as a focal point in their new home. I had no knowledge of my new client or any idea of their lifestyle and preferences. Instructions were given to me by their designer regarding the size of the piece and the selection of colours for the interior scheme. Desperate for a clue or trigger for an image, I used the first syllable of the family name as my subject! There were five members of the family — so I used five rams but do not conclude from this that they were all male. I had great fun combining a group of quite disparate fabrics in the construction of these noble animals. It involved juxtaposing standard velvets with otherwise ugly pieces of real "Persian lamb" and mock astrakhan. It is useful to keep a limited supply of unusual fabrics because when used in conjunction with other more conventional cloths they help to make an interesting mix. For an outrageous contrast to the somewhat staid colour of the rams I chose gold lurex and metallic fabrics for their horns in an attempt to elevate them from ordinary breeders to fine decorative creatures of substantial pedigree.

Eyes are always an important feature of my work. I believe they should follow you around the room!

PROJECT

HARE WASTEPAPER BIN

This elegant wastepaper bin is constructed very simply by stretching and glueing a giant ribbon or strip of appliquéd cloth around a drum. I used thick industrial cardboard tubing employed in the building industry to form concrete columns. It is usually available from building suppliers and sometimes from better craft shops too.

The cylindrical form of this object creates a three dimensional illusion to the appliqué greatly enhancing the image of this chic black larger than lifesize hare.

I chose a combination of strong dark colours as well as the predictable pastels so that this beautiful bin could reside in a study or library as easily as milady's boudoir or powder room.

Think about the possibilities of co-ordinating the fabrics on a bin like this with your upholstered furnishings or bed coverings. You may have some fabric off-cuts you can incorporate in your design to facilitate an inexpensive result. Small animals like squirrels, monkeys, cats and dogs have an obvious and often personal appeal for an object such as this. However you could be just a bit more adventurous and make a weasel, stoat, fruit bat or skunk bin!

Directions:

Start by assembling the backing piece. The background for the hare loosely represents sky and ground with a slim padded strip between the two on which the hare is placed. The padded strip is 1.5cm (three quarters of an inch) wide and is 4cm (1 and a half inches) from the bottom of the bin. Use fabrics and colours of your choice for the backing. There will be plenty of leftover fabric, top and bottom, to form a lining for the interior of the bin.

Read the *How To Do It* chapter on page 29 and enlarge the pattern using the grid system as explained on page 30 with 1 square = 2cm (three quarters of an inch). Cut out and assemble appliqué according to the basic instructions and step-by-step guide. To place the first hare, find the centre of the backing piece by folding it in half, 86cm (34 inches) sides together. The tip of the nose is placed at a point which is 13cm (5 and a half inches) up from the padded strip and 7.5cm (3 inches) from the centre fold line. For the second hare, flop the placement and the cutting out pattern (the stitch-and-tear is transparent enough for the pattern lines to show through on the reverse side) and cut out and pin design elements to the mirror image of the original.

Position second hare and satin stitch it to the backing.

Wrap the tube with the appliqué, ensuring that the hares are displayed well. With a pencil, mark the overlap of the backing on the exterior of the cardboard tube and squeeze white glue on the line. Press one edge of the backing onto the glue. Squeeze another line of white glue onto the fabric's edge and press the other edge of the fabric onto the line of glue. Hold the glued seam in place until dry with drawing pins.

Mist the interior of the tube with spray

Note:

The directions are for a cylindrical bin 38cm (15 inches) high with a diameter of 33cm (13 inches) which is decorated with a pair of 32 cm (12 and a half inches) tall appliquéd hares facing one another with their noses15cm (6 inches) apart. For a bin of a different size and shape, the pattern, measurements and materials will have to be adjusted accordingly.

If you want to have the two hares facing one another as I did, remember to flop the pattern (turn it over to get a reverse image) for the second one.

You will need:

Sufficient stitch-and-tear (lightweight non-woven backing) for four full size patterns of the hare; Spray adhesive; Selection of fabric scraps plus pieces large enough for the body and hindquarters; Fabric for backing, pieced together to measure 107cm (42 inches) x 86cm (34 inches); Dacron batting; Plastic headed pins, multi-coloured; Selection of machine threads; White glue; Drawing pins; 90cm of 25mm (1 inch) wide Petersham (grosgrain) ribbon; Cardboard for bottom and interior lining.

adhesive and press the excess fabric above and below the hares smoothly onto the sprayed surface. Glue and pin the vertical seam on the inside as well.

When the glued seam is dry, remove pins and glue Petersham ribbon over the seam for a neat finish. Fasten with drawing pins until dry.

On the cardboard, scribe a circle with a diameter matching that of the inside of the bin. Before cutting it out, add four tabs, spaced evenly, to the outer circumference. Cut out the circle with the four tabs attached. Cut a strip of cardboard to line the interior of the bin, covering the fabric. Position the circle 5cm (2 inches) above the bottom of the bin using drawing pins to fix it at the four tabs to the inner sides. Bend the strip of cardboard into a tube and insert it in the bin. Fix with drawing pins if necessary.

BIRDS

COUNTLESS ARTISTS HAVE MADE THE STUDY OF BIRDS THE MAJOR FOCUS OF THEIR LIVES...THE BIRD IS USED AS A SYMBOL OF PLACE AND NATIONHOOD.

The great 19th-century American artist John James Audubon spent his working life painting over a thousand life-size figures of birds, each in their particular environment, surrounded by foliage, flowers, fruit and insects. When you consider that this painter spent a lifetime illustrating birdlife in the forests, swamps and river valleys east of the Mississippi, it is easy to be daunted by the wealth of material available in birdlife everywhere else.

Reprints of ornithological illustrations from centuries past are still produced today — such is the popularity of birds and their environments. Countless artists have made the study of birds the major focus of their lives. With many species facing imminent extinction this is probably just as well. Like flowers, birds are used as symbols of place and nation, such as the American eagle and the bird of paradise for Papua New Guinea. The ultimate symbol for all mankind is the dove of peace which Pablo Picasso drew so simply. My earliest recollections of birds in a domestic decorative context is a set of five ceramic ducks that adorned the living-room wall of our family home. They were painted in the appealing colours of the male mallard including the white band around the throat. Each bird was slightly smaller than the last so that you could either believe they were flying away from you in fright or towards you in wild anticipation. I thought they were the best things ever and secretly still do. Nowadays I realise that the study of birds in the arts would require several lifetimes to record and appraise.

Late in the 1970s I was approached by a New York firm of Chinese American architects to create a classic American cocktail bar atmosphere in my home city of Melbourne. What a cocktail! My client had incorrectly determined that the only decorative wildlife Australia could provide was the black swan and that it should be surrounded by lotus flowers. Now the black swan is certainly unique to Australia, but it is also the symbol of Perth, a city on the other side of the continent, and seldom seen gliding through lotus flowers. The client is always right, of course, and so I accepted the Black Swan Bar commission.

The architects' concept for the room was very stylish. My applique panels covered the walls from floor to ceiling. The images were appliqued onto the same cherry red velvet in which all the chairs were upholstered.

A totally enveloping environment was created where even the doors had to be covered with applique! The brief was very clear. The colours for the room would be red and

Cartoons for the Black Swan Bar are the final working drawings at mural size from which the calico patterns are traced.

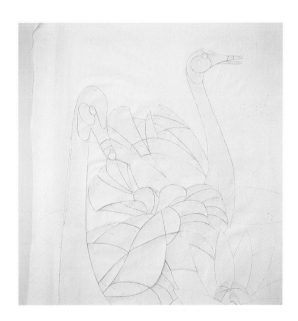

black and the only other colour could be in the lotus flowers on the lily pads. Initially this seemed very restricting but quickly became my first intriguing experience of working with a single colour palette — black. Since then I have used this black with indigo to create a dense richness of colour in other works like the dress in 'Tissot and Mrs Newton'.

The Royal Melbourne Botanic Gardens are home to many pairs of black swans and their families and I spent an enjoyable day at the lake photographing them from almost every angle. My amateur photography provided the basis for the black swan images. These were finally edited back to five and positioned on alternating panels or in mirror image across and around the walls of the octagonal room. The narrow panels allowed for a small detail from a group of lotus or a single swan. The considered placement of the large images around the room helped retain the architectural integrity of the space by achieving a sense of formality.

Two calico tracings are made. The top copy is cut up into pattern pieces and pinned back into original position on the uncut tracing to await the colouring process.

Lotus blooms and pads are coloured, backed and awaiting placement on the cherry red velvet.

The service bar presented a major technical problem. Clearly lush cherry red velvet and overflowing cocktail blenders are not compatible. I used a theatrical device and replaced the lower half of one panel with a cherry red mirror. The effect of the appliquéd swans and flowers over the mirror is very luxurious and one that I had developed with success some years before. I had now reached the stage where the jig-saw of coloured shapes had been completed and the swans were padded up and ready for stitching when the client phoned to say the scale was too big! Could I please make them at least one third smaller. Three months work was discarded, the cartoons were re-scaled, new patterns were made and we started it all again. In retrospect the architects made the right decision. It's just a pity they did not make it earlier.

I liked this little black swan from the bar and decided I had to make more of her.

Folding screens are useful pieces of furniture as well as being decorative. Six panels, each more than two metres tall and half a metre wide, make up this lorikeet screen. In the Australian bush the lorikeet is as vividly coloured as the South American macaw. I chose to ignore this fact and created this mega-parrot screen based on old-fashioned rose colours — pinks, creams, mauves and purples — colours not usually associated with parrots. My concern was for the overall feeling and mood of this screen using the bird shapes interacting with one another rather than a literal representation of lorikeets — an option still available to me in the unlikely event that I should ever decide to repeat this work.

The soft colours of this work belie the beady eyes of the birds.

The bright colours
employed on this screen
are for effect and are
not an exact portrayal
of a genus of parrot.

Full tropical flush of
feathers, beaks, baubles
and fan palms.

The strength of these
macaw images ensures
no further need for
decoration.

This macaw screen is a very strong and dramatic piece of work. As with all my folding screens I have used the system of a formal pattern by repeating the image back and forth across a number of panels. This simple scheme creates new patterns of colour and shapes when the screen is viewed from different angles.

When designing folding screens, consideration should be given to the fact that rarely will the whole screen be seen at one time. Often it will be behind other furniture and only the top half seen. Some panels may even be completely obscured at certain angles. I think of folding screens as backdrops against which people can enjoy their domestic environment.

The colours I chose for this screen are vivid — real parrot colours. Outrageous jungle greens and screaming tropical sunsets — are not colours suited to everyone's taste! This is real exhibitionism. The sort of work an artist creates to make a big impact.

The colours used in the construction of these fabulous birds are far from being ornithologically correct. It is not necessary to be a slave to nature. It is your idea, impression or interpretation of the image that makes it your own. If you want real macaws you must go to South America.

The technique and finish in this early screen does not bear close examination. The birds and flowers have been sewn together prior to being attached at their edges to the backing cloth — hence the wrinkled result. For a near perfect finish all stitching of any image should be made through to the backing cloth prior to placing and stretching over a frame or panel. Fortunately these flamingos and flowers are so spectacular their owner failed to notice my learning curve.

There are eight exotic birds on this screen with only twelve legs between them — it's a miracle.

PROJECT

TEA POT COVER

'Only a bird in a gilded cage' — is just fine if the cage is really a tea cosy and the bird is an appliquéd image! Hopefully caged birds are a thing of the past.

This table decoration is a sort of appliqued fabric sculpture or *trompe l'oeil* in cloth. Made with a fine sense of whimsy, this tea or coffee pot cover is intended to enhance your table setting and provide a conversation starter at afternoon tea when you could be entertaining the Lady Mayoress or your local vicar. "Tell me vicar — do you prefer your canary in or out of it s cage?"

Clearly this design is created to encourage you to use colours that might complement your napery or crockery and complete the table top vista. Maybe a white bird in a silver cage worked on a pale pink background could be your interpretation of this simple image where the satin stitching actually forms the wire filigree for the cage.

The shape of this fabric cover has been designed for standard size tea pots but with a small extension to the base of the cage it could become a cover for a coffee plunger or pot.

You may prefer of course to replace my canary image with that of the exotic toucan or a tiny wren, depending upon the atmosphere you wish to create and the environmental awareness of your guests.

Note:

Firstly, measure your tea pot. The finished cover here measures 32cm high x 28cm wide (12 and a half x 11 inches). To make the cover wider, simply add an equal number of birdless segments to both sides of the pattern, shaping them at the top to accommodate the broader curve. If using velvet as I did, cut some of the pieces on an angle to give the work even greater variety in tone and texture. Make two appliqués (one for each side of the tea pot cover) and instead of attaching each assembly to backing fabric, stitch it to lining fabric of the same size as the pieced appliqué. The handle is made from eight segments of fabric glued over a small polystyrene ball the size of a ping-pong ball.

You will need:

Sufficient stitch-and-tear (lightweight non-woven backing) for four full size patterns ; A selection of fabrics for the appliqué and ball handle; Dacron batting; Lining fabric for the tea pot cover; Yellow machine thread and gold metallic thread; Small polystyrene ball for the handle; White glue.

Directions:

For the actual appliqué to be 35.5cm (14 inches) high (a hem of 4cm (1 and a half inches) is turned up to give the cover a stable base), enlarge the pattern using the grid system as explained on page 30 with one square = 2cm (three quarters of an inch). Make four copies of the pattern; you will use two for each side.

Read the *How To Do It* chapter on page 29 and cut out and assemble the appliqué according to the basic instructions and step-by-step guide. Be generous with the mistings of spray adhesive so that the assembly is well secured before you start using the sewing machine.

Remember that the background fabric in this case is a lining for the tea pot cover.

When satin stitching, remember that in order for the golden 'bars' to contain the canary, they must be sewn after the bird. In this case, the order of work is - bird first, then bars and cage bottom.

After assembling both pieces, seam them around the sides and top, right sides together, stitching a scant 1cm (half an inch) from the edge. Turn up the bottom hem and catch it in place by oversewing the lower section of the bars, again using the metallic thread.

To make the ball handle:

Use a long needle and generous length of strong thread to make a stitch through the centre of the ball and back down again so two ends of the thread can be later used to anchor the handle to the top of the tea pot cover.

Cut out eight curve-sided segments of fabric, each one 1.5cm wide at the centre and 6cm long, from the pattern supplied. Glue them to the ball shape with white glue making sure that the anchoring threads are swinging free. When the glue is completely dry, insert the anchoring threads in two needles and stitch through the tea pot cover top and secure threads firmly on the lining side.

FISH

THE CORAL REEFS OF OUR WORLD TEEM WITH SCHOOLS OF FISH IN BRILLANT HUES WHICH COULD ONLY HAVE BEEN CONCEIVED BY A DERANGED COLOUR CONSULTANT.

It is not uncommon for people to ignore the wonders of their own environment. How many Americans have visited the Grand Canyon or Parisians the Eiffel Tower?

It was with some trepidation that I made my first visit to the Great Barrier Reef off Australia's north eastern coastline. I was not expecting such a major experience. Every artist should visit a coral reef and try to absorb some of what nature created under our oceans. The patterns and colour of the coral formations, the bewildering array of invertebrates including molluscs such as trochus and helmet shells, cowries and giant clams, crustaceans and worms of science fiction proportion are all stunning inspiration. Then there are the fish! Over 1500 species inhabit the waters of the Great Barrier Reef. Teeming in their thousands, darting shapes of intense colours and patterns flash through shafts of sunlight then dissappear into the azure-blue infinity. No theatre or movie can create such an astonishing bombardment of colour and pattern — a myriad eyes peering at you from timid faces painted in every hue. It is truly another world.

The coral reef is an ideal source for my imagery as I am primarily concerned with colour and shape — lots and lots of the same thing. It may be roses piled high in a Florentine market or multi-coloured shipping containers stacked like building blocks. The concept of one object repeated many times and thereby creating wonderful patterns always fascinated me. It was inevitable that I should find such satisfaction in the masses of colour and shapes in the waters of the Great Barrier Reef.

*These massed shapes
require great patience
in construction
and sewing.*

*Basically a study in blues
and purples this piece
could be made again
in any number
of colourways.*

Schools of crazily patterned fish with carnival mask-like faces presented a real challenge to my patience during the construction of these appliqué works. The fish arrive as a wall of colour, assaulting the senses and numbing the mind. So many shapes are almost the same that it is difficult to differentiate between them as they dart off emitting sporadic flashes of silver and gold.

I decided that in order to make the viewer aware of the tropical location in which these fish live, I would put palm trees in the background. This was easily done and gave a sense of balance to the picture which it had previously lacked. However something still worried me about the overall image. I went back to my photographs and realised what it was. Palm trees are not common among Australian flora and except for a few holiday resorts are rarely seen. But by then it was too late.

These overscale fish work well in this image. There is no relation to size or scale.

Caught in a shaft of sunlight, these batfish flaunt themselves briefly before moving off.

Although it extends over a huge area, most of the Great Barrier Reef is within the Marine Park, a World Heritage Site that is zoned to prevent over fishing. Partly as a result of this, the fish are remarkably tame, as curious of visitors as we are of them.

Batfish are typical schooling fish often appearing to act as escorts to the visiting diver.

With faces like under-
water harlequins, these
tropical fish dart across
the picture frame.

VELVET ENVELOPE BAG

Bright blue starfish found washed up on the shore while walking along a deserted beach, inspired this simple and very sensual velvet bag. I combined velvet of the palest sandy beige with the vivid ultramarine of the starfish for the outside of this fabric envelope and contrasted them with a luxurious taffeta lining to suggest its use as a harbour for precious jewels or luxurious lingerie.

The random placement of the design allows for as many or as few starfish as you desire but remember that in positioning them you should consider the bag when it is both opened and closed. Although it is a fairly fiddly procedure, you should try to keep as much wadding behind the starfish shapes as possible so as to ensure a strong sculptural feel to these exotic underwater creatures.

Starfish have quite vivid colours in their natural habitat but there are no rules in the textile arts so you can make your starfish whatever colour you fancy.

If starfish do not appeal to you consider using other marine creatures. You can choose from a breathtaking array of shells or even little fish would look amazing on a blue-green sea coloured bag. Once you have decided which image you want to use, restrict yourself to a selection of sizes. Do not try to crowd your work with too many shapes and colours.

Note:

The pattern given is for an envelope 37 x 24cm (14 and a half x 9 and a half inches) with five starfish on the flap and a single starfish on the lower front. As each starfish motif is stitched separately to the bag they may be positioned as you choose. The method is simpler than that which is described in the *How To Do It* chapter on page 29 but as the techniques of using stitch-and-tear and spray adhesive are the same, read the chapter before you begin.

You will need:

Sufficient stitch-and-tear (lightweight non-woven backing) for one full size pattern of starfish; Spray adhesive; Fabric for starfish; Fabric for envelope at least 40 x 76cm (16 x 30 inches); Lining as for fabric; Dacron batting; Plastic headed pins; Machine thread to match starfish fabric.

Directions:

Enlarge the pattern using the grid system as explained on page 30 with one square = 3cm (1 and one eighth inches).

Using the enlarged pattern, cut out one each of front and back with flap for bag from each of fabric and lining and one of back with flap from batting.

From the enlarged pattern trace the starfish shapes from both front and flap of back onto stitch-and-tear. Cut out the shapes and pin them to a pin board covered with newspaper. In a well ventilated room, spray the pinned-on pieces with adhesive. Take each shape and place sticky side down, on back of starfish fabric and press with a warm iron. Cut out each starfish shape which is now faced with fabric.

Cover the pinboard with a fresh sheet of paper and pin on the shapes, stitch-and-tear side up. Mist with adhesive as before then press each shape, sticky side down on spare batting. Cut out shapes so each is backed with batting.

Arrange the starfish shapes to your liking on the front and flap of the bag fabric, remembering there is 1cm (half an inch) seam allowed. Mark positions with pins and remove shapes. Mist the batting side of each shape with adhesive and press into place at pins.

Satin stitch through all layers following instructions for the order of work on page 30. Try to keep as much batting behind the starfish shapes as possible, using a pin to push back any stray bits as you stitch.

With right sides together, join lining to front along top edge, stitching a 1cm (half inch) seam. Turn right sides out, press and top stitch close to edge.

Matching bottom edges, place right side of front to right side of back and pin side and bottom edges and stitch.

With right sides together, place lining over back and flap then arrange batting on wrong side of lining. Pin together then stitch around, leaving an opening of about 15cm (6 inches) in centre of bottom edge.

Turn to right side through opening, turn in raw edges and stitch opening.

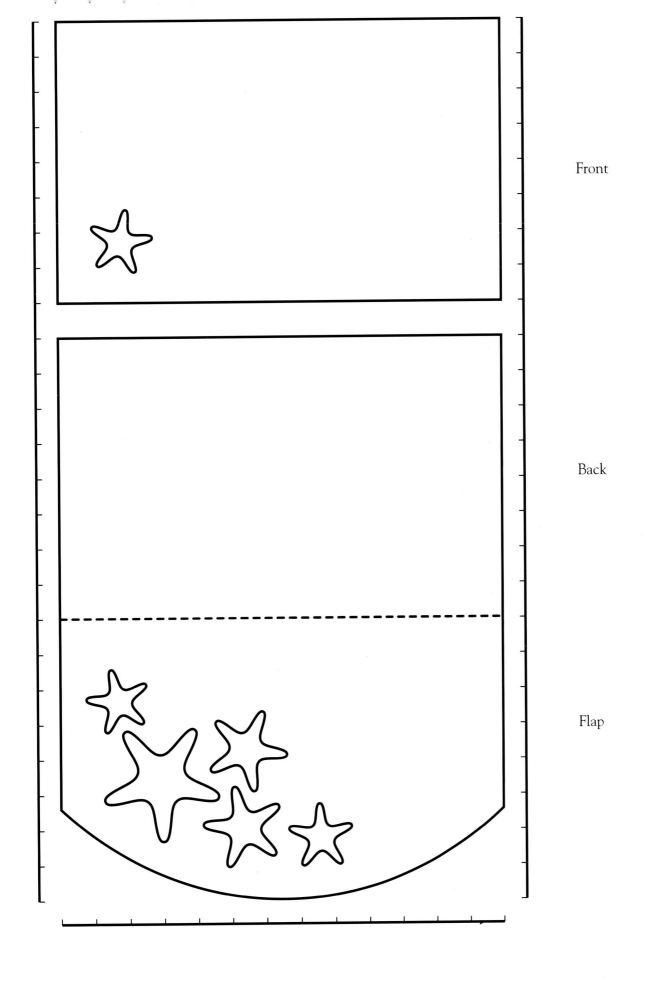

Front

Back

Flap

SHOWBIZ

THERE IS ANY AMOUNT OF IMAGERY IN THE PERFORMING ARTS FOR EVEN THE MOST DOUR OF SOULS TO DRAW ON.

There's no business like show business — and it's true! The performing arts in every form have always been a source of inspiration and intricate association for textile artists. Costumes, curtains, cycloramas and decor of endless imagery and fantasy have been created with textiles appliquéd, beaded, painted, dyed, torn, tucked, embroidered or simply draped in colourful cascades through the centuries. They have been an integral part of comedy, tragedy, circus, cabaret, opera, music hall and dance right up to the explosion of today's electronic entertainment.

The ancient Greeks started it all with their classic chorus of elegantly draped figures and Busby Berkley was still doing it in the 1930s in a more frivolous fashion. There is any amount of imagery in the performing arts for even the most dour of souls to draw on. My choice seems to be images from the stylish and symbolic characters of the *commedia dell'arte* and the high camp colour of Molière's theatre of 17th century France. Contrast these with the traditional performance arts of Japan and say the Indonesian island of Bali, and you quickly understand the infinite breadth of inspiration the performing arts supply to the visual artist. A study of the mask as a decorative and symbolic device would provide more work and inspiration than any one lifetime would allow. In this electronic age we are bombarded with a zillion images which we mostly discard as quickly as we receive them. Maybe it is the responsibility of the visual artist to capture and celebrate some of these fleeting images and freeze them in time for some future generations to consider. What images will replace such icons as Marcel Marceau, Marilyn Monroe or Miss Piggy, I wonder.

Groucho's striped pants
incorporated fabric
normally used for
neckties.

*The beautiful silk taffeta
used to create the frock
and gloves probably
cost more than the
original ones.*

These two works were created with a real sense of purpose. Both are one and a half metres square and believe it or not, give directions to visitors as they step out from the lift on the fifth floor of a major office building. To one side is a diamond merchant, signified by Marilyn Monroe in her legendary frock and diamonds, doing her 'diamonds are a girl's best friend' routine. There is a temptation with a work of this sort to incorporate crystal beads to create the diamond choker and bracelets but I am a believer in keeping the technique of appliqué as pure as possible and making the fabrics and threads provide the image. The addition of extraneous materials often turns major pieces into crafty dustcatchers.

Groucho Marx on the other side of the foyer, points the way to a very large Jewish travel tour operator. He makes the perfect foil for Marilyn in his blacks and greys with the only spot of colour being the boutonniere which I made out of the same silk taffeta as the blonde star's gown. I was proud and delighted with the result of these two signs and appreciative of a client who never questioned my judgement in this commission.

Groucho Marx was a clown in the classic sense. He created a performance face in much the same manner as a circus clown would prepare his mask. Nobody really thought that Groucho went around every day dressed as a cross between an ambassador and an undertaker. This was his adopted persona just as Charlie Chaplin or Marcel Marceau had theirs. With a little study it is usually possible to draw the faces of these famous performers using those instantly recognizable features which are their trademarks.

I was very aware of these traditions when I constructed this work of Groucho and it made what is a usually difficult task much easier. His spectacles presented the only real problem.

*Bored, blowzy, Berlin
broads pretend to ignore
the louche lounge lizards
who surround them.*

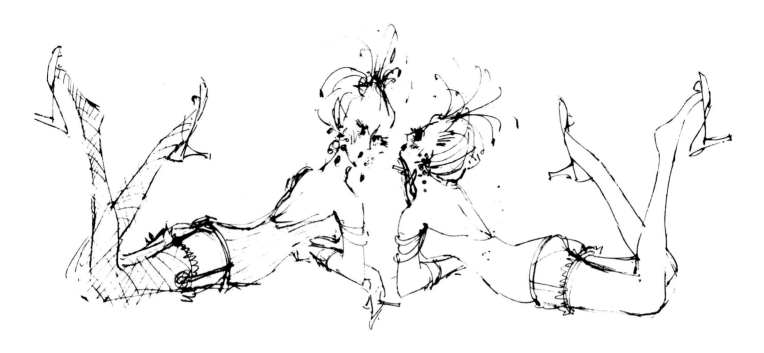

*Original presentation
drawings for the client.*

*Calico patterns patiently
waiting for their colours.*

*Cabaret girls in the
process of receiving
their colours.*

This was another night club commission for which I had planned an enormous non-stop frieze of Berlin cabaret girls bumping and grinding their way around the room. One continuous line of legs and bottoms with satin pumps dangling on their toes ready to be kicked off into the thrashing throng of the club's exuberant clientele. But unfortunately this was not to be. Even as I was ordering the first hundred metres of pink satin the client had second thoughts and slashed the budget. Instead of sixty seductive sirens they cut me back to six panels strategically positioned around the room. Hopefully some of the mood of pre-war Berlin with it's wild cabarets and acid political satire, so well described by Christopher Isherwood in his novels and in the movie *Cabaret*, still comes through.

Strangely enough I modelled her legs on those of a male friend with whom I was sharing a studio. They seem very elegant.

I was interested in producing a substantial work that actually denied the picture plane — something that broke away from the surface and shape of a panel but still related back to it in some way. This 'showgirl' mirror which is over two metres long was my way of breaking out of the mould.

I felt sure that I could make an image of the stereotype of showgirl in appliqué because her intricate and exaggerated costume would be as sensational as my technical skills would permit. The colours I chose were pink on pink underlining the fleshy idea of the subject. I next decided to perch her precariously on the frame of a rose coloured mirror like some gorgeous feathered creature. Since the life of a showgirl is all reflections, artifice and feathers it seemed appropriate!

The subject of this work bears no resemblance to my 'Berlin broads' on the previous spread. This lady does not speak — she is just there to be ogled by all and is obviously suitably recompensed!

Technical considerations when making this piece were considerable. Not only did I need to take her costume and the contoured areas of her figure into account but also the construction requirements for those crucial points where the image meets and becomes part of the frame.

This was an early work and I would be nervous about taking on something as technically demanding again.

The lady above welcomes visitors to the lobby of the showroom at the casino in Alice Springs in central Australia.

Some friends suggested that this image was intended to be a self-portait but I don't think I have ever looked like this and certainly I have never owned the costume. However I understand their perception. In another life I would happily have taken on the role of court jester or fool philosopher — being part of everybody's life and yet nobody's. Being there for the important moments and absent for the rest. Pointing the way yet being left behind and still content.

In Shakespearean plays the fool was a recognised commentator and I suppose today his part is often taken by creative people. Possessions prove nothing. The act of creation is rare. The saying used to be 'plant a tree, write a book, have a son' and apart from the sexist attitude to progeny, the concept still holds true. But I digress. When I was commissioned to create something for a birthday celebration I indulged myself with this reclining harlequin. It is about two metres long and is a strange combination of Castro man and traditional clown. His hat is probably a bit extreme but since there was no reference for this work I should not expect everything to be perfect.

The trapunto technique has been wildly exaggerated in this poor jester's cap.

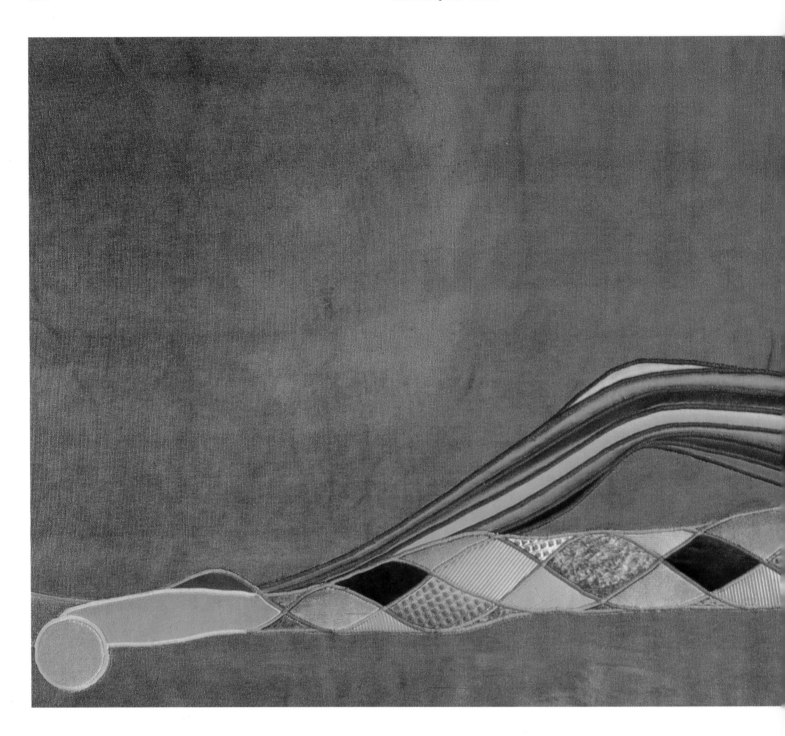

The fool, the jester,
the philosopher. You
notice the colours and
hear the voice but never
see the person.

*The balloon is
echoed in the
pom poms and collar
of this Italian clown*

This traditional character bears a sad burden, symbolised by the balloon.

This stylish pair of *commedia dell'arte* clowns are each more than two metres tall. Their costumes, which are seen at full length on the preceeding pages, use black, white and blue with one red as the only bright colour. The background material was a 'brown paper' coloured velvet.

The final width of these panels is dictated by the maximum width available in the background fabric. This is always a major consideration when constructing large pieces and often the image has to be carefully designed to hide joins in the cloth.

It does seem that the more advanced the state of our civilization, the less colour we have in our lives. Somehow primitives have much more style than moderns and yet we think we are the ones who know everything!

The minstrel comes from a sequence of images I developed to symbolise the arts in general. All of the characters are harlequin figures and they are either writing, dancing, painting, or playing a musical instrument. This is the only character that I have completed in appliqué to date, but hopefully I shall eventually find the time to work through the rest of them. The panel is one and a half metres in length and is really a study in red and black. The placement and choice of texture in this work is very simple and I hope effective. Satins and silks make up the balletic shirt and velvets are used for the tights and pom poms on his slippers and costume. I allow the ideas of circles and stripes to run on through the image — circles for the instrument, slippers and shirt and stripes from the minstrel's hat through the ruffle collar and on to the sleeve and tights.

*Black patent leather
was used for the face of
the lute. Not the sort of
material one would
normally choose to stitch
alongside delicate satin!*

The background of colonnade and elephants was completed before Eartha and her howdah fans were positioned for stitching.

This was a real bedroom farce! Almost five metres in length, this extraordinary work was commissioned as a bed head. It was designed to cover the wall above a huge bed and its adjacent bedside tables with the big elephant's ear drawing the whole fantasy together. The subject matter for the imagery was demanded by the existing statuary and furnishings in the large and luxurious suite together with my recent enjoyment of the brilliant cabaret artist Eartha Kitt in the Broadway production of Timbuctoo—a scandalous black re-make of the original Kismet.

The work took more than three months

to make and the client came round to check progress several times during it s production. On completion it was so large that it had to be hoisted by crane over a balcony and through the French windows but all went well and delivery was effected in one piece. Once installed, the client decided she would like one of the background velvets changed because the colour varied from one end of the bedhead to the other. No amount of explanation from me about the nap of the cloth and the play of light could alter her determination and the client is, after all, always right. Back I went to the nuptial suite, wrenched the work from its frame (by this time I was in a foaming fury) and tossed those months of work into the back of my small car like a bundle of dirty linen. Weeks later I started the difficult task of unpicking all the satin stitching and changing the lower background cloth from pale gold to dove grey. At this stage the interior decorator decided that the new colour changed the look of the room too much and could not go back. Would I please store the work indefinitely. I suspect that the client had not informed her high-flying husband that his sanctuary was about to be invaded by a herd of elephants and was too terrified to do so.

SLEEPING MASK

Showbiz can be all about searching for a star and working nights. This heady combination takes its toll on those who fall under its spell. Their need to sleep during those hours when everyone else is awake necessitates the frequent use of a sleeping mask. Unfortunately the lights and noise of our modern cities have created a need whereby many of us, who seldom work nights, also need to wear sleeping masks to ensure our rest is undisturbed.

Modern travel has also altered our sleep patterns. As our bodies hurtle across the world in jet planes, the use of sleeping masks has grown to become a vital item to help cope with changing time zones and the inevitable circadian disrhythmia. What was once only part of a movie queen's accoutrement is now an accepted feature of our everyday lives.

This small object makes a perfect gift and can be personalised in a million ways. The star of your show would have to wear this one made simply from gold and indigo velvets. A contrasting binding or thread would change the look of this mask completely.

Because this is a very small object it is sensible to choose simple imagery for best results. Try a silver lamé semi-quaver on a midnight background for your jazz musician lover who spends his nights thrilling his fans instead of you!

Directions:

The pattern is the correct size (no need to enlarge it but the grid has been included in case you want to use the stars for another project) so trace over it and from the tracing cut out mask from main fabric, from lining and from batting.

Trace the star shapes onto stitch-and-tear. Cut out the shapes and pin them, right side up, to a pinboard covered in newspaper.

In a well ventilated room, spray the pinned-on shapes with adhesive. Take each shape and place, sticky side down, on the wrong side of the star fabric and press with a warm iron.

Cut out each star shape which is now faced with fabric.

Arrange the star shapes to your liking on the right side of the mask, remembering that the binding will cover about 6mm (quarter of an inch) around the edges. Mark positions with pins and remove shapes.

Cover pin board with a fresh sheet of paper and pin on shapes, Stitch-and-tear side up, and mist with adhesive as before.

Press shapes in position on mask.

Satin stitch around edge of each shape following instructions for order of work on page 30.

Sandwich batting between mask and lining with right sides out and pin together.

Cut two 50cm (20 inch) lengths of bias binding, place wrong sides together and stitch close to both long edges. Thread elastic through the tube formed, stitching across both ends to secure.

Matching raw edges, pin elastic strap to lining side of mask. Adjust for fit and stitch across each end close to edge, trimming any excess of strap.

Bind edges of mask with remaining bias binding, turning in raw ends neatly.

Note:

As each star motif is stitched separately to the mask they may be positioned as you choose. You may decide on another motif altogether. The method is simpler than that which is described in the *How To Do It* chapter on page 29 but as the techniques of using stitch-and-tear and spray adhesive are the same, read the chapter before you begin.

You will need:

Sufficient stitch-and-tear (lightweight non-woven backing) for the star or other motifs; Spray adhesive; Selection of fabric scraps including at least 20 x 10cm (8 x 4 inches) for mask and the same amount of soft fabric for lining; Lightweight Dacron batting; Plastic headed pins; Selection of machine threads including gold for stitching stars; About 30cm (12 inches) of 10mm-wide (three eighths of an inch) elastic; 1.5 m-wide (59 inches) of 12mm (half inch) bias binding.

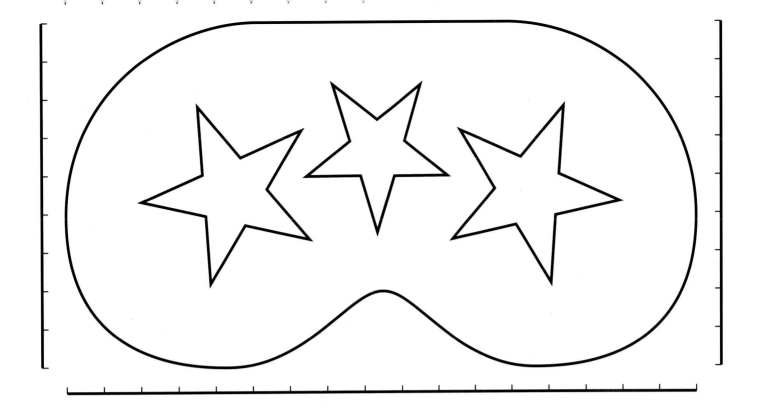

PEOPLE

THERE ARE INFINITE INSPIRATIONS TO BE GAINED FROM ALL PEOPLE...OF BODY AND CLOTHING, SIZE AND SHAPE...THE SMALLEST AND SIMPLEST STATEMENT OF ANY CHILD.

For many artists, mastering the human form has frequently been a lifetime journey of discovery and despair. I well remember having this shocking realisation during my very first life-drawing class at art college when I was confronted by the large, pink, naked form of a woman and told to draw her. It was hard to believe my crusty lecturer's statement that this moment was to be the beginning of a lifetime challenge. He was right of course and I have since wasted much of my time trying to take short cuts with little success. No matter how hard and long one tries to perfect a drawing of the human form there will always be another nuance and subtlety to discover.

Textiles are an intrinsic part of our lives and until the recent introduction of space-age foil we were wrapped in cloth at birth and again at our exit. People surround their lives and bodies with textiles for their clothing, homes, work and rituals. Textiles bear witness to our most intimate moments and it is as well that they cannot talk.

One might first be encouraged to create an image of a person by the clothes they are wearing, such as the intricate and bejewelled vestments of a Russian Orthodox priest contrasting dramatically with a dogmatic face. Or perhaps the simple shape of a bedouin woman captured starkly against a landscape of tent and sand with little to be seen of her face other than shadows.

All peoples provide a source of inspiration: simple things such as combinations of body and clothing, size and shape, place and purpose through to the untold moments of their history. These may be the monumental and historical or perhaps the smallest and simplest statement of any child — just being and possibly wondering why.

Despite the abundance of frangipani flowers in this image, your attention is still drawn straight to the face.

Try your hand at a simple portrait of a friend or family member and include their pet or an indication of their hobby or pastime as a whimsical addition. Perhaps even as a major element. Do not enslave yourself to producing a perfect likeness — just create an attractive and amusing image and you will be astonished by the response from other people.

After an unexpected holiday in the remote and dreamy islands of Tahiti I was so enchanted that I felt I needed a record of those wonderful people. Handsome muscular men wearing leis and crowns of tropical flowers came as a strange contradiction to this foreigner with my pale and stitched up heritage. However I was soon to understand their freedom and balance and decided to celebrate this feeling in my work. I thought I was being very bold in my choice of fabric for this man and made sure that I did not hide his chest by having his frangipani lei attached only at his shoulders.

The face of this man standing in the crystal clear waters of his island home seems to echo the mask of an ancient and primitive culture.

The face of Lady Why
exudes a sense of another
place and time.

Experienced,
determined and maybe a
visionary. This is the
Lord Admiral.

For years I had ignored the request of friends to make a work for their home as I am always nervous about friends and finances. However as needs must and also because of their persistence, I eventually relented and the very large pair (1.5 metres tall) of which these two faces are details, was the result.

My idea was to create two seemingly formal portraits but which were in fact an amalgam of some of the features of my friends plus a lot of fantasy. Added to that was the whimsical overlay of the poached egg on the shoulder of the Lord Admiral and the blue wren on the shoulder of the Lady Why, which kept everyone guessing. These works although quite self-contained and able to stand alone were conceived as a pair to be hung alongside one another so that the coastline behind the subjects flowed and symbolised their independence. My friends live in an expensive beachside suburb — hence my choice of the coastline as a background.

The face of Lady Why is pretty and blonde but she exudes a sense of another place and time. For his part the Lord Admiral suggests great experience, determination and the inevitable short-sightedness, although he sees himself as a visionary. Why does the lady have her fingers crossed and where is the Admiral's left hand?

Made in pastel silks and satins, this image reflects the repressive formal wear for children in the Victorian era.

This delicate image which I gave the title of Byegone Child is approximately one metre high and comes from the inner reaches of my subconscious. It is an image which from time to time appears to me without any apparent cause. Friends suggest that it was an expression of my grief over the loss of my daughter Zoe, but I prefer to see it as a simple statement of innocence and youthful beauty.

I consciously chose to make this work in pastel silks and satins with an obvious reference to the cumbersome formal wear which children were forced into during the Victorian and Edwardian eras. A time when clothes seemed calculated to bind up and repress the natural joy and energy of youth despite the shocking hypocrisy of the parents. I intended this work to reflect the simple unadorned beauty of a young person.

Working in appliqué to construct a face can often be awkward as the cloth can pucker unexpectedly and thereby add years to the age of the subject. I deliberately kept the face of the Byegone Child extremely simple so as not to interfere with its beauty and innocence. Some textile artists paint over the material to achieve the desired result but I prefer to live with the purity of the initial applique technique.

Constructing an appliqué face requires great care as any small pucker of the material may add years to the age.

How an angel found its way into a chapter on people puzzles me but since there is insufficient material for a separate section called Myths and Fantasies she is allowed to stay. The angel now resides in a private function room in a luxury casino where hopefully she is able to improve people's fortunes.

The work was purchased from one of my very early exhibitions by an interior designer who was seeking to complete an exotic fit-out. It is not one of my most successful images for a number of reasons. Were I to attempt it again I would treat the subject in a far more imaginative way. Also the rippled satin background was not intended and came as a clear lesson not to use cheap or inferior fabrics on large and important shapes (unless of course you are seeking the rippled effect!).

By partially covering a face with a lock of hair, little can go wrong.

This angel lives in a casino where she guards the fortunes of the players.

However my association with the purchaser ultimately developed into a sound professional relationship and several large and exciting commissions ensued.

One way of overcoming the difficulties of making faces in appliqué is to cover them over or break up the open areas of the face with other shapes such as jewellery, hats, shadows, scarves or, as in this case, with hair. All the emphasis is placed on the working and colour mix of the hair with just a profile and exaggerated eyelash and brow shapes creating the face. In this manner there is little that can go wrong but if you do see a problem another lock of hair might just cover over your mistake!

*It would be helpful if
all faces in appliqué
could be resolved as
simply as these
Egyptian musicians.*

This mural is made up of three panels, each a little over one metre square. It was commissioned by a designer for an anonymous client on the strict understanding that its owner would never be revealed. This touch of mystery has certainly enhanced my own feelings for the image.

The very simple brief for the work was to create a mural around the colours cream, coral, turquoise and black. This colour palette suggested an Egyptian theme to me so I sought architectural reference before starting the project. Many of the images found in Egyptian murals are quite inappropriate for a peaceful domestic scene which is why I chose gentle figures of clothed musicians and handmaidens, laden with jewellery and other decorations. By mirroring the two end panels I have given the work some formality as well as framing them with my interpretation of classic Egyptian ornamental motifs.

Imagine how striking it would be to extend this idea around the walls and doors of a restaurant or even a private dining room. One of the highlight colours could be used on the tables and chairs and another for the floor.

The two dimensional nature of these images echoes the feeling of this ancient period.

The simplicity of Egyptian mural paintings and ornaments enables an easy transposition to the medium of textiles.

The face of the old woman orange vendor demonstrates how, with only the fewest of lines and shapes, a clear and simple image can be made.

Like most people, the time available and my physical abilities to complete projects often fall well short of my enthusiasm and ideas. This work was to have been the first in a series of images of street vendors but alas this orange seller was the first and last. She was inspired by any number of people and stalls in Europe and other parts of the world and is the result of a number of photographs.

My intention had been to make a study of massed colour of fruit, flowers or vegetables as well as a more complex treatment of the vendors themselves — a sort of up-to-date textile artist's interpretation of the Hogarthian theme. You will notice that the face of this gentle woman uses very few lines yet it is clearly an older face. This effect is helped by the choice of faded fabric for her face and hands.

The landscape behind the orange vendor could have been anything from a fruit market to a horse and cart, but I chose the easy way of creating an almost abstract background. I did this by placing together a collection of broad sweeping shapes in earthy colours to suggest a landscape rolling away to a winter's sky. It is not always necessary to impress your audience with your appliqué skills when the best solution to a problem may well be the easiest.

*Oranges and other citrus
fruit contrast strongly
with the dull surrounds
of the fruit market.*

A pair of satin covered cushions made for effect rather than use.

This is a pair of very large tailored cushions entitled 'Fan Tan Fannies'. They are 750 mm square, very crisply finished and of course completely impractical. I had a fixation on creating a mirrored image using a white satin face emerging from a white satin background. They were all very graphic and frightfully clever but a total nightmare to sew without marking and impossible to use in real life. Anyway here they are and I hope the reader likes them as much as I do. They reproduce beautifully in the pages of this book and this should probably have been the limit of their use. The same image worked in other colours and fabrics would be a much more practical solution but it would not have given me the opportunity to send myself up to the same degree.

Like much of my early work in appliqué, this image began as a tiny thumbnail sketch which I enlarged straight up to finished size so there is a very simple and direct feeling about it. I planned these big tailored slabs to be the top cushions on two stacks of perfectly plain black ones — the furniture equivalent of a stack of Chinese food containers with their cloisonné or lacquered lids on top. I thought this could be the start of a whole new thing to make the textile arts more accessible. I'm still thinking about it!

SPECTACLES POUCH

So often we spend frantic minutes searching for our spectacles in their tasteful leather case. In fact the case is so tasteful that it has disappeared amongst the surrounding domestic clutter. Do not deny the reality of your spectacles. Celebrate them! Make them easy to find in a crisis. Appliqué this spectacles pouch boldly and brightly so that even in the wildest panic it demands your attention.

I chose to state the obvious on this design by creating a classic pair of sexless spectacles to decorate the surface of the pouch. The colours are more fashionable than they are alarming, and would certainly be an ac-ceptable gift for any man or woman.

Use this design to create your own colour combinations. The perfect gift solution for the one-eyed sports fan is to make this design in the colours of the club which they so vehemently support. If the grandparents are becoming fractious, make it up to them in lovely soft shades of velvets and taffetas, re-flecting their silvering hair and warming their gentle hearts.

Party queens would adore their specta-cles hidden away in a pouch as black as night with this design worked in gold, pink and silver lurex!

Note:

The pattern for the pouch is cut out of what is usually called the backing fabric. In this case, because the design appears on this piece, it is referred to as the front. Follow the directions and pattern given here or use an existing pouch as a model.

You will need:

Sufficient stitch-and-tear (lightweight non-woven backing) for two full size patterns of the appliqué; Spray adhesive; Selection of fabric scraps including at least 30cm (12 inch) square for pouch and the same amount of lining fabric; Light weight Dacron batting; Plastic headed pins; Selection of machine threads; 90cm (36 inches) of 12mm (half inch) -wide bias binding. Press stud.

Directions:

Enlarge the pattern using the grid system as explained on page 30 with one square = 1.2cm (half an inch). To make pouch pattern, trace over enlarged shape noting the fold line which is the fold line on the front for the flap and the cutting line for the back.

Cut one each of front and back from main fabric, lining and batting. The front is the background fabric for the appliqué.

Trace the spectacles pattern directly onto stitch-and-tear making two copies.

Read the *How To Do It* chapter on page 29 and cut out and assemble the appliqué according to the basic instructions and step-by-step guide. At step 14, position spectacles on the front of the pouch. When stitching, complete the wings before doing the frame.

Sandwich batting between front of pouch and lining with right sides out. Pin together and stitch around close to the edge.

Repeat for back of pouch. Bind straight edge of back with bias binding.

With wrong sides together, pin front to back and stitch around close to edges. Bind all edges of pouch with remaining bias binding, turning in raw ends neatly.

Fold flap to back and apply press stud to close flap.

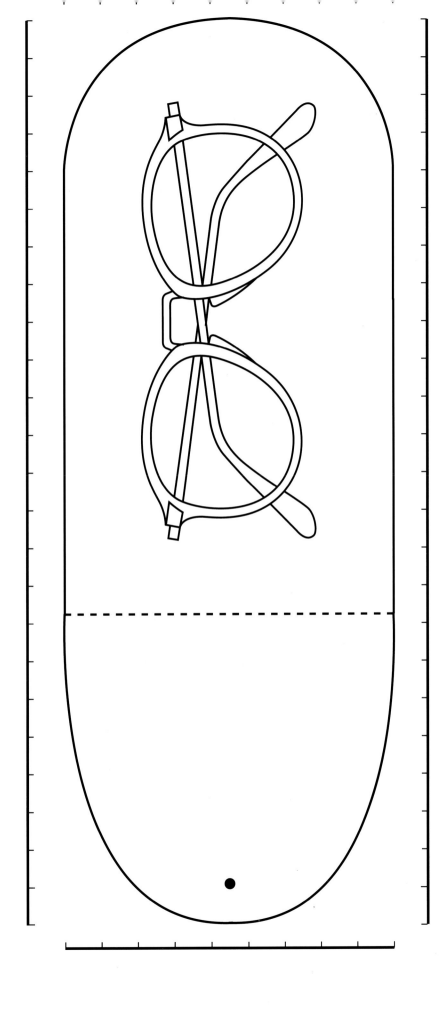

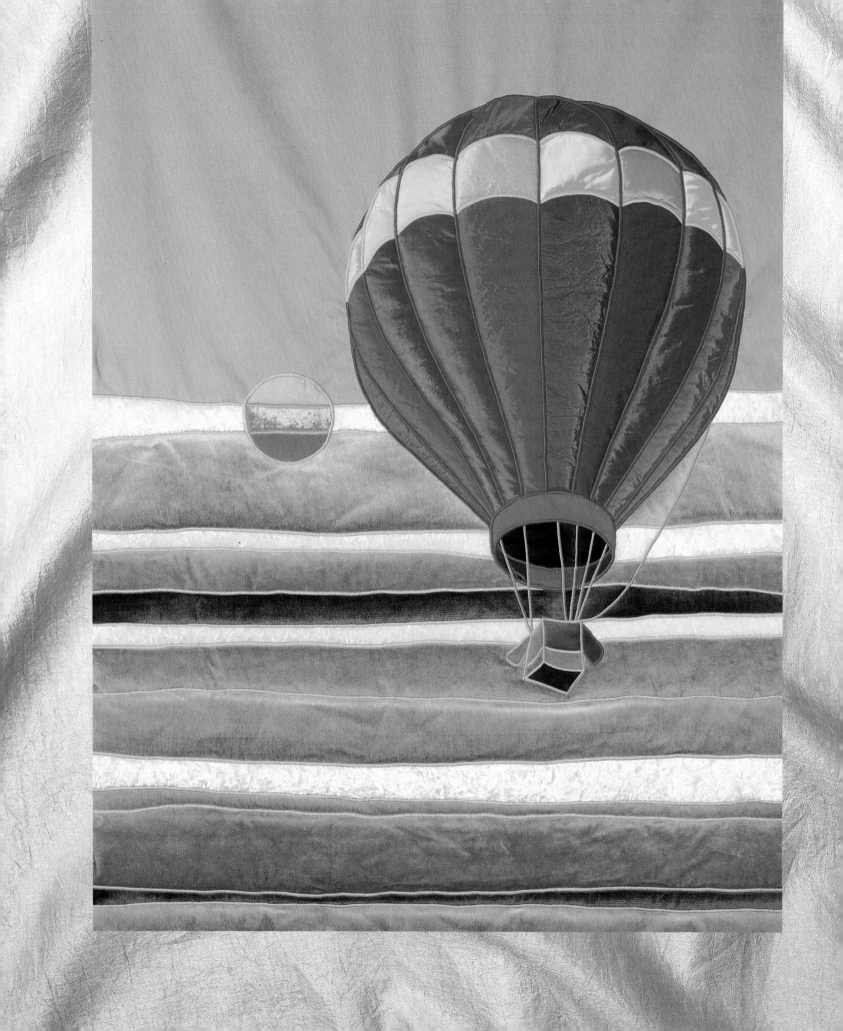

SPORT

IT IS THE IMAGE MAKER'S DELIGHT TO MARSHALL TEAMS OF BRIGHTLY DRESSED BODIES MASSED IN ACTION OR REPOSE.

The sporting world has always been a great source of involvement and inspiration for the art of appliqué. Ever since knights in shining armour set out with banners unfurled on thundering steeds draped in stunning colours, appliqué has been used to identify and unify sporting teams. Today both team and individual, become ever more spectacular as heroes, clubs and corporations clamour for immediate recognition on the sporting stage. The textile arts appear everywhere in print, embroidery and appliqué and whether we like it or not, brand names and corporate logos have become an integral part of everyday life.

It is the image maker's dream to marshall teams of brightly dressed players massed in action or repose. A creamed team of cricketers set against a bright green playing field and a clear blue sky with only the bright red of the cricket ball as a highlight, is a perfect example. For an artist daunted by the fluoro-coloured attire and equipment of other sports, cricket, croquet and bowls are an excellent canvas.

The gentle sport of hot air ballooning was my introduction to the world of aeronautics. A series of bright banners was commissioned by a travel company to hang in their vast booking hall—an enormous street level space in a glass tower block. Primarily they were conceived to be public art with a clear reference to the client, but secondly, and almost as important, they were to help humanise the scale of the space and absorb the sound. This is not a new concept. Banners have served this purpose for centuries in the cathedrals of Europe. I used the old 'freeze frame' technique with the hot air balloon moving further and higher into a peaceful summer sky—combining symbols of peace and freedom.

The sport of ballooning
lends itself to the spirit of
appliqué with its rounded
forms and colourful
parachute silks.

When Jacques and Joseph Montgolfier sent up the first hot air balloon in 1783 they initiated one of the most colourful sports of all. According to contemporary sketches of the event, that first balloon was brilliantly decorated with images reminiscent of the toiles which had been introduced just twenty years earlier. The next balloon which went aloft unmanned came down in a small market town just north of Paris. There it so frightened the local people that they attacked it s silken folds with guns and pitchforks, completely destroying it!

Despite this initial reaction, the advantages of balloon travel gradually came to be recognised and by the turn of the century people were being transported at reasonable speed and in great luxury over considerable distances. Then came several major disasters with gas filled balloons and their use went into a swift decline.

Recently however, ballooning has returned to the greater safety of the original hot air concept and the popularity of this sport is once more on the rise. Now you can glide over Australian deserts, float over French vineyards or drift silently past groups of African wildlife, safely suspended in your wicker gondola. These rich, silken images for a major travel company gave me great pleasure to make.

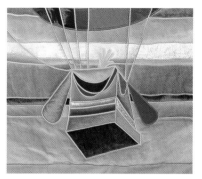

A subtle touch of humour in one of the hangings is this hand extending from the basket.

The texture of parachute silk adds a three dimensional effect to these balloon murals designed for a modern travel office.

*Lifesaving clubs begin
recruitment at a very
early age.*

A lifesaving carnival is a parade of youthful beauty seen regularly on the surf beaches of Australia. Clad only in luminous swimming costumes, these bronzed young Australians are part of the beach attraction for international visitors and have instigated such annual events as the Iron Man competition and the Surf Board and Ski championships. The openings and closings of these events are attended by club teams wearing their formal all-in-one body suits, marching behind their captains who carry large banners with their club's ensignias. Great blocks of wonderful colour move across large stretches of golden sands with crashing seas and clear blue skies as a backdrop.

The graphic use of the safety colours yellow and red on a lifesaver's cap feature again on the large flags he positions on a beach. These are for surfers to recognise as the area which is safe for swimming and which is constantly patrolled. This unique sport provides the visual artist with a wonderful combination of sun, sand, sensuality and astonishing clarity. Combine the primary colours used in this sport and its ruggedly beautiful venues with the superbly crafted surfboats and the surfboards, skis, inflatable dinghies, flags and crowds of onlookers. It is no wonder that many artists are seduced by this sport of the sea.

*My image of a
lifesaver in his formal
one piece lycra suit is
unusually tame for its
choice of colour.*

*A sailing enthusiast
commissioned this work
for which silks, satins
and taffetas were the
obvious choice.*

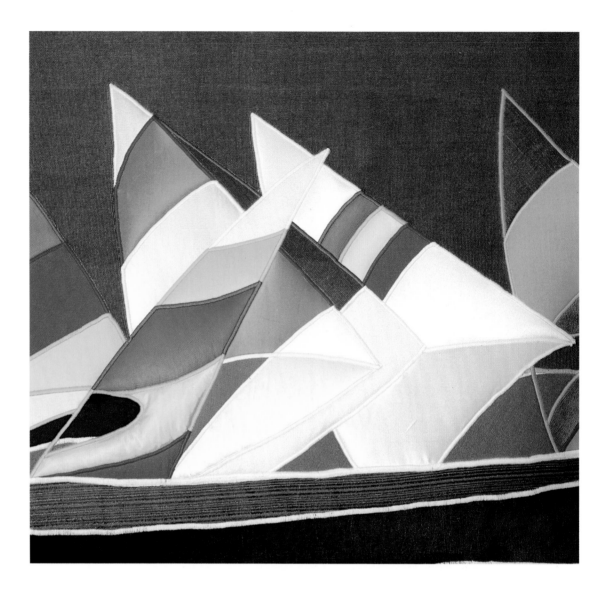

'Windsurfers' is a large work that was commissioned by an enthusiastic sailor for the wall of his luxurious tower block apartment overlooking the rolling waves of the Pacific Ocean.

The work consists of one panel nearly 4 metres in length which required a crane to deliver it over his balcony and through the living room windows. At his request I incorporated the colours of his sail as a major element in the work. It is the very large one appearing to win the race on the left side.

There is no need for me to explain the suitability of windsurfing or other types of sailing for the making of imagery with textiles. One has only to look across any accessible piece of water with even the faintest breeze to be assured of the sight of hundreds of square metres of gloriously coloured sails thrashing, billowing or gliding across the horizon.

Colours and shapes change and glow in the sun like a living kaleidoscope. Silks, satins and taffetas were an obvious choice for the sails in this very colourful appliqué panel.

Some years ago after a visit to London where I saw a wonderful exhibition of the works of Raoul Dufy I returned to Australia with my head full of the colours used by this famous French painter and designer. A number of his works incorporated images of both French and English racetracks and seeing the purity and brightness of his colours I was inspired to incorporate some of them into my panel of jockeys. These are two from a set of four panels, each 1.25 metres tall. The design of the silks for each rider is based on the four suits in a deck of playing cards. These striking panels were commissioned to enhance the wall of an executive lounge in a horseracing organisation. As well as the vivid green of the race track and the jockeys' silks and caps I have used a combination of metallic lurex golds to construct the winning trophies. Their breeches are a study in different white satins and silk with the creases defined by the white cotton of the satin stitch. The riding boots and goggles are a combination of different vinyl, leather and patent leather fabrics. Even the whip handle is made of sturdy brown leather to add verisimilitude for *aficionados* of the track.

The world of horseracing will always provide a limitless supply of subject matter for images, patterns and designs for any artist.

*The problem of depicting
the jockeys' faces is
overcome by goggles,
caps and horses' heads*

CLUB COLOURS

Imagine this muscle flexing lifesaver in your sporting club's colours. You may even know a sporting friend who would be proud of this design featuring their club colours casually tossed amongst a group of cushions on the couch of their family home or beach house. This design enables you to use any number of club colours in the surrounding frame of the image on to the swimsuit of the lifesaver.

You may wish to incorporate a sporting club logo, graphic or mascot on his swimsuit and feature the club colours on his cap.

Sporting colours are all about clarity in identification so don't be afraid of going too far with your creative ideas. If you want to have a green sky and a yellow sea behind a lifesaver who in turn is wearing a yellow and green cap — do it! Don't hold back. Let your viewer know who you are cheering for. Any sport can be used in this way if you choose a simple image like a tennis racquet, a cricket bat, a bicycle or any of the thousands of obvious items of sports equipment. The idea of different balls used in the various sports with their respective goals or nets gives a starting point for an easily recognisable design — a soccer ball and goal, a basket ball and net or a baseball and glove are a few obvious examples.

The choice of which sport and what colours is already made for you when you know who will be the proud recipient.

The directions given are for a 50cm (20 inch) cushion with optional piping. The appliqué itself measures 40cm (16 inches) square.

You will need:

Sufficient stitch-and-tear (lightweight non-woven backing) for two full size patterns of the lifesaver; Spray adhesive; Selection of fabric scraps; About 1 m (1 yard) of fabric for backing, cushion back and bias trim; Dacron batting; Plastic headed pins, multicoloured; Selection of machine threads; 2.1m (2 and a half inch) cushion insert.

Directions:

For the applique area to be 40cm (16 inches) square, enlarge the pattern using the grid system as explained on page 30 with one square = 2.2cm (seven eights of an inch inch).

From the main fabric, cut two 52cm (20 and a half inch) squares one for backing for appliqué and the other for back of cushion. From the remainder, cut sufficient 5cm (2 inch) wide bias strips to make at least 210cm (82 inches) when joined.

Read the *How To Do It* chapter on page 29 and cut out and assemble the appliqué according to the basic instructions and step-by-step guide. Be generous with the mistings of spray adhesive so that the assembly is well secured before you start sewing. When stitching, complete the background sections first then the foreground, arms and facial features.

To complete the cushion, fold the bias strip around the piping cord, with right side out and stitch close to cord, using zipper foot of machine. With right sides together, pin bias strip around edge of appliqué backing piece, matching raw edges, easing around corners and unobtrusively joining ends. Stitch in place, sewing over stitching line. With right sides together, pin back of cushion in place, matching edges and stitch over stitching line, leaving an opening in one side. Turn to right side, push the cushion insert through the opening, making sure the corners are well in and slip stitch the opening.

It is hard to imagine a
group of real people
having a picnic beneath
gold lurex palms.
Maybe this is as far as
one can go with colour
variations.

LANDSCAPES

CREATE YOUR OWN LANDSCAPE BY TAKING WHATEVER ELEMENTS YOU ENJOY AND ARRANGE THEM IN YOUR VISTA OF DREAMS.

"Beyond the blue horizon waits a beautiful day!" We all know that the words of the song are a dreadful lie — and thank heavens for that. Our planet would be a very boring place if we were forced to enjoy blue skies everywhere we went. The meaning of landscape is as wide and varied as nature and your imagination can create. Anything and everything is possible. What was once considered to be a fantasy may now be well understood as just another moonscape or perhaps the result of global warming. Allow your senses to create your own landscape by taking whatever elements you enjoy and arranging them in your vista of dreams.

In many people's minds the word landscape implies a tradition of a scenic view rearranged and reproduced with a frame around it and hung neatly on some poor wretch's living room wall. Landscape can be anything from the size of a matchbox to an enormous mural of a 360° vista covering all the walls in a large public hall.

In the world of the textile arts one only has to join together two different coloured cloths horizontally and you have created a landscape — an empty vista of land and sky or water and sky upon which you can place as many or as few elements as your artistic passion desires. My favourite, and the first element I usually add, is a nice circle for the moon or sun. This creates the anchor for my design and depending upon its chosen position on the picture plane I add my other selected elements. Quite often the texture and colours of the different base cloths create their own suggestions and direction for the subject matter and the feeling of the finished piece.

*Where have the
picnickers gone? In for a
swim or up one of the
palm trees?*

*Originally included only
as a point of focus,
the picnic has since
become a talking point.*

*(over)
This work 'Pelican
Beach' is basically the
same landscape with the
sun repositioned and all
but the thermos and
tumblers removed from
the picnic due to the
sudden arrival of one of
my favourite birds.*

This never ending saga of oasis picnics
began with the large panel opposite. The
group of palm trees with the deck chairs beneath was originally included only as a point
of focus and to balance the setting (or rising)
sun, since which time it has reappeared by
request in many different guises. You will
notice that, unlike the grande dame editor of
American Vogue magazine who strictly for-
bad her staff to include palm trees in any
fashion pictures, I adore them! I use them
often in different colours and configurations.
To my mind they are a clear phallic symbol of
strength and growth — pushing straight up
from the earth and exploding with their abundance of food and shelter.

You may prefer to fill your landscapes
with motor vehicles, buildings, rocks or cafes.

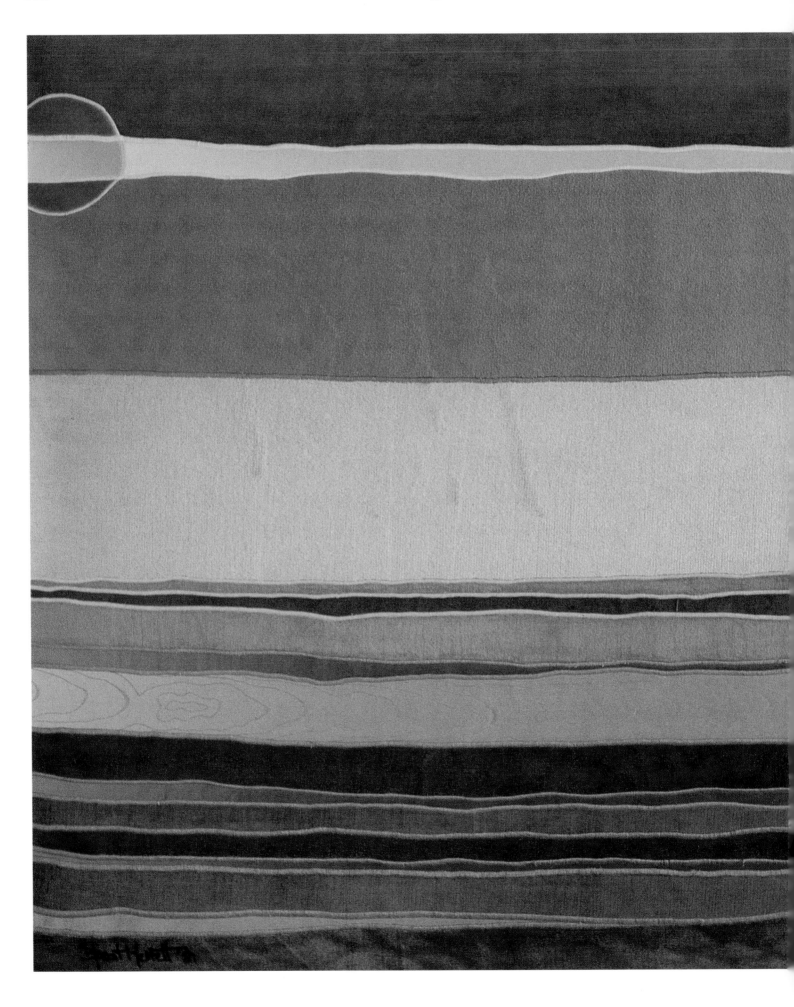

The trick of foliage over (or through) this circle affords simple fabric colour changes that become exotic rainforest sunset detail.

This is Biggles the biting cat, guarding the front door.

Doors, entrances, archways and stairs all lead somewhere. They beckon and entice you to enter and explore what is behind and beyond. Consider an exhibition of works based solely on images of many different entrances to buildings — strange, wonderful or even boring doors surrounded by architecture and ornament.

This work entitled 'Biggles the biting cat' is 1.3 metres tall and is my first attempt at a collection of doorways. Who amongst us is not keen to know what lies behind the many facades we pass daily. One often discovers the most unexpected horrors behind a superb Georgian entrance or conversely the most detailed and exquisitely fashioned interior through a dilapidated doorway in some Morrocan alley.

This work gives a hint of the warmth behind the big panelled door and a glimpse of a lushly carpeted stairway reflected in an oval mirror. The marmalade cat at the pavement called Biggles awaits the arrival of visitors so he can greet them with a sharp bite on the ankle. A cat that did not attend charm school!

Architecture of all periods and places whether in a landscape or in isolation provides a bountiful source of inspiration for the visual artist. Look through any window and discover a landscape.

Door detail from one of the largest applique commissions I have ever undertaken.

In looking for superlatives, I think this appliqué facade made up from nine panels and measuring almost five metres in height could be one of the largest works of appliqué in the Southern Hemisphere. It was commissioned for one of those modern buildings whose tenants' occupations and professions are many and varied. As usual, I was desperate to find a suitable image for the foyer and all I could see was a blank space. However after some research I discovered that the site on which the new building stood had originally been home to a brewery called McCracken & Company. Searching through the phone book I eventually made contact with a member of the McCracken family and subsequently obtained a black and white etching of the original brewery building. Research is always interesting providing you can find the answer!

The choice of colour in this work is a blend of architectural reference and artistic license. One stroke of fortune was when I came across some strangely water-stained terracotta velvet which I used for the red brick walls on the first and second floors of the building. This added extra interest for 'close inspectors'.

The pair of pigeons on the mouldings near the top of the work may well have been the progenitors of the flocks of pigeons that now desecrate so many of our historic buildings.

Almost 5 metres in height, this work was commissioned for the foyer of an old building which had been renovated and converted into modern offices.

These trams (or streetcars if you prefer) are working relics of a byegone era and still transport the people of Melbourne along their tree-lined boulevards. Now famous as symbols of their city, these old warriors are under constant threat of being derailed by 'high-tech' models designed in Italy or Scandinavia.

Despite being famous as a tourist attraction they will eventually have to make way for their modern descendants in the interests of safety standards. I am pleased that I was commissioned to make this large panel as a celebration of Melbourne transport before they departed from the scene.

This work is entitled 'Peak Hour' and is approximately four metres in length. It graces another grey space — hopefully allowing the viewer to enjoy it s play of shapes and colour instead of anxiously watching the elevator indicator.

This panel is almost the maximum size that one person can manage through a sewing machine without help from an assistant.

Most works of this scale and larger should be made up of smaller panels thereby ensuring proper control of the sewing process. Another advantage of smaller panels is that the weight of the finished piece is manageable.

*Great care was taken to
ensure that the sails of
the yachts all point in the
right direction.*

*The Sydney Harbour
Bridge in real life with
the Opera House just in
view top left.*

This work should really be called a cityscape rather than a landscape. It covers the famous vista of the Sydney Opera House, Circular Quay and the Harbour Bridge — a vast panorama that I would not normally attempt except that I received a commission by telephone one afternoon and away I went.

An old copy of National Geographic Magazine supplied me with a suitable aerial shot of the scene that I was requested to reproduce and I developed the image from that. In a work of this nature it is easy to become bogged down in the intricacies of the subject matter so I endeavoured to simplify everything as much as possible and allowed the fabrics and the threads to tell the story.

At one stage I thought this could become an enormous magical mural using minute architectural details together with historic and social references inset in the relevant areas but sense eventually prevailed.

The ocean liner berthed at Circular Quay and the yachts sailing under the famous bridge, often referred to disparagingly as 'the coathanger', give the work a sense of scale.

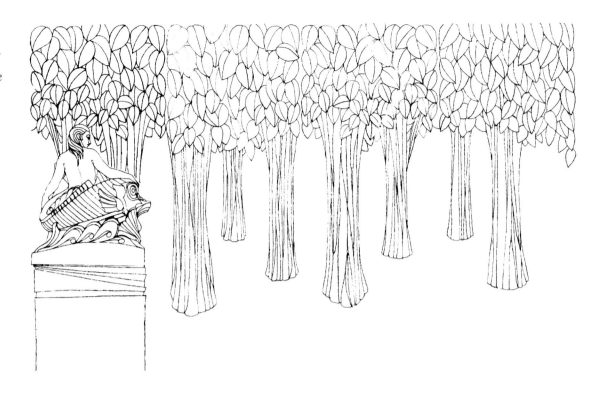

Original drawing for the mural showing the two sculptures at the entrance to Fitzroy gardens.

Statues often provide emotional land-marks to which you return all your life. Typical of these would be Peter Pan in Kensington Gardens, the Little Mermaid in Copenhagen harbour and Alice in Wonderland in New York's Central Park.

Even a maze takes on a life force and meaning for those who visit and enjoy its challenge and beauty — a stolen kiss behind a hedgerow that started a dynasty!

'Mermaid and Fish' in sculpture (right) and as conceived in appliqué (above).

These two large murals , each six metres long by three metres tall, enabled me to celebrate two sculptures to which I have a great attachment. They hang in the lounge adjoining the lobby of a Hilton hotel and I felt it important that the images helped the patrons relate to their external environment, since so many of these venues have developed their own international anonymity.

The Fitzroy gardens just opposite the hotel are populated with large English elm trees which are fast becoming rarities in the rest of the world due to the ravages of a fungus-carrying beetle. The entrance to the gardens is announced by this pair of unusual statues 'Boy and Pelican' and 'Mermaid and Fish' by the sculptor William Leslie Bowles. I have simplified the complexity of the landscape by concentrating only on the black textured trunks and the vivid green leaves of these enormous trees and the statues on their pillars.

It was my intention to highlight the beauty of this pair by using them separately in each mural and thus force the viewer to consider their wonderful forms.

'Boy and Pelican' in sandstone (above) and fifty years later in applique (left).

PHOTO ALBUM

How many of us have wonderul old books in our homes that we really do not know what to do with? They are so old and out of date they make hopeless reading but the quality of the paper and the binding make them too good to throw away. Nobody wants to buy them so why not cover them with colourful appliqué designs and use them as coffee table 'startlers' and paperweights. Once you have a couple of these big numbers lying around there will be no need to purchase expensive fashion magazines to fill the gaps on your coffee table. You could pretend that you are a member of the Secret Service and hollow out the pages of one of these thick, gilt-edged tomes, leaving about

2cm of readable pages at the outside edges. Instead of smuggling state secrets you can cover the book in exquisite appliqué and then use it as a very special storage box.

Apart from these decorator suggestions you could also consider recovering the family bible or historic photo album maybe using a crest or monogram surrounded by a formal border. Create a beautiful wedding album as a gift to a happy couple, using images of orange blossom, doves, ribbons or even a fabulous wedding cake made in pink and white satin.

Should you feel daunted at the prospect of covering the book with your appliqué, seek a craftsman bookbinder to finish the task.

Note:

The pattern given is 16 x 23cm (6 and one quarter x 9 inches) and will suit most photo albums. If you wish to change the size of the appliqué to suit another book, enlarge or reduce the pattern using the grid system as explained on page 30. If you intend to have a professional bookbinder to cover your book, make inquiries about the size of backing fabric you should use and where to place the appliqué.

You will need:

Sufficient stitch-and-tear (lightweight non-woven backing) for two full size patterns; Spray adhesive; Selection of fabric scraps; About 50cm (half a yard) of fabric for backing to cover the album; Dacron batting; Plastic headed pins, multi-coloured; Selection of machine threads; Sufficient heavy paper or lightweight cardboard to cut two pieces the size of the inside of the cover.

Directions:

Measure the fabric required to cover your album. It may be easier to make a paper pattern and mark on it the placement of the appliqué strips you wish to place on the spine. Remember to allow at least 5cm (2 inches) to fold over the edges.

From the main fabric, cut out the cover piece and mark position for appliqué.

Read the *How To Do It* chapter on page 29 and cut out and assemble the appliqué according to the basic instructions and step-by-step guide. Be generous with the mistings of spray adhesive so that the assembly is well secured before you start sewing.

When stitching, complete the background sections first then the foreground.

Cut out and stitch any strips for the spine in the same way.

Try the completed cover on the album and mark position with pins for accurate placement. Mist the album with adhesive and place on cover carefully. Trim excess fabric from corners and fold the edges around the cover, spraying more adhesive if necessary. Cut two pieces of cardboard for inside covers about 1cm (half an inch smaller) all around. Stick in place with spray adhesive.

ACKNOWLEDGEMENTS

The publishers would like to thank the following people for making their photographs available for this book.

Simon Blackall
4, 6, 12, 13, 26, 27, 28, 30, 32, 33, 48, 54, 64, 66, 92, 94, 102, 104, 124, 126, 140, 144, 146, 152, 153, 160, 162, 178 left, 179 right, 180, 182.
Mario Borg
10, 21, 38, 39, 40, 41, 42, 43, 44, 45, 46, 56-57, 58, 59, 60-61, 62, 73, 76, 77, 82, 84, 85, 86, 87, 111, 112, 113, 114, 115, 116-117, 122, 123, 128, 130, 134, 135, 136, 137, 140, 142, 143, 154, 155, 156, 164, 166, 167, 168, 169.
Earl Carter
8, 74, 75, 99.
Mark Goyen
100.
Norton Hobson
14, 17, 18, 22, 23, 24, 25, 96, 98, 106, 108, 109, 110, 148, 149, 150, 151, 172, 174, 175.
Ian McKenzie
36, 37, 49, 55, 68, 70, 71, 72, 88, 89, 90, 91, 118, 120, 170.
Stewart Merrett
138, 139, 171, 176, 177.
Vanessa Robb
46, 121, 131, 132, 133, 157, 178, 179.

INDEX

Italicised entries denote either the title of a work or that it is illustrated on that page.

LIST OF WORKS

Title page. Detail of waterlilies from mural in Black Swan bar. Regent Hotel, Melbourne.

Imprint page. Detail from topiary roses, 1988.

Page 9. Encore! 1993, 2m x 1m. Exhibition piece.

Page 10. Tissot and Mrs Newton, 1981, 2m x 1m. Collection of the artist.

Page 14. Framed Fruit, 1989, 75cm x 75cm. Collection of the artist.

Pages 17,18. Framed Fruit, 1988, Variations on a theme. Private collection, London.

Page 19. Prickly Pears, 1984, 2m x 1.2m. Private collection.

Pages 20, 21. Prickly Pears, 1984, 2m x 1.2m. Private collection.

Pages 22, 23, 24, 25. Heritage for Visions, 1989, 6 panels, each 2m x 1.5m. Order of Saint John of God, Ballarat, Victoria.

Page 25. Celtic Pomegranate, 1989, 2m x 1m. Order of Saint John of God, Ballarat, Victoria.

Pages 26, 27. Cherry Bags, 1992. Collection of the artist.

Page 28. Framed Pears, 1992. Exhibition piece.

Page 34. Detail from Iris Screen, 1982.

Page 36, 37. Iris Screen, 1982, 4 panels each 2m x 0.5m. Private collection, Western Australia.

Pages 38-39. Strelitzia Reginea, 1982, 2m x 1m. Private collection.

Page 41. Geraniums, 1985, 2m square. Private collection.

Pages 42-43. Cyclamen I, II, III, 1982, 50cm x 70cm. Private collection, Myrtleford, Victoria.

Pages 44-45. Waterlilies, 1985, 2m x 1m. Private collection, Melbourne.

Page 46-47. Topiary Roses, 1988, three panels 2m x 1.5m. Private collection.

Page 49. Daisies, 1980, 1.2m x 60cm. Private collection.

Page 51. Arum Lilies, 1980, 1.5m x 1m. Private collection, Victoria.

Pages 52-53. Arum Lilies, integrated panels 6m x 1.5m. Installation, Casino Restaurant, Darwin, Northern Territory.

Pages 56-57. 'Elizabeth Taylor's Gift', 1981, 2m x 60cm. Private collection.

Page 57. Strap Cactus, 1981, 1.2m x 1.4m. Collection of the artist.

Pages 58-59. Daffs, 1980, 1.2m x 0.5m. Private collection

Pages 60-62. Floral Emblems, 1988, each 50cm in diameter. Collection of the artist.

Page 63. Sturt Peas, 1985. Ogilvy & Mather, Adelaide, South Australia.

Page 64. Hippeastrum, 1992, 1m x 1m. Exhibition piece.

Page 68. Zebras, 1980, 2m x 1.5m. Private collection, Sydney.

Page 70. Orang utan, 1980, 1.2m x 50cm. Collection of the artist.

Page 71. Giraffes, 1979, 1.5m x 1m. Private collection.

Page 72. Hippos, 1981, 1.5m x 1m. Private collection.

Page 73. Possum on Banksia, 1984, two panels, each 1.5m x 1m. Private collection.

Page 74. Great Grey Elephant, 1986, 1.5m x 2m. Collection of Tennyson Graphics, Australia.

Page 75. Great Golden Elephant, 1986, 1.5m x 2m. Private collection, The Hague.

Page 76-77. Merinos, 1988, 2m x 1m. Private collection, Victoria.

Page 78. Hare waste paper bin, 1992, 50cm x 1m. Exhibition piece.

Page 82, 84, 86. Black Swans, 1982, four panels each 2.5m x 2m. Installation, The Regent Hotel, Melbourne.

Page 86. Black Swan Frieze, 1980, 2m x 0.8m. Private collection, Melbourne.

Page 87. Lorikeets, 1984, four panels of screen each 2m x 0.5m. Private collection.

Page 88-89. Macaws, 1986, three panels each 1.5m x 1m. Private collection, New York.

Page 90-91. Flamingos, 1980, Screen of four panels, each 2m x 0.5m. Private collection, Hong Kong.

Page 92. Tea pot cover, 1993, approx. 40cm high. Exhibition piece.

Page 96. Angel Fish, 1990, 2.3m x 1.5m. Private collection, Daydream Island, Queensland.

Page 98. Tropical Fish, 1990, 2.3m x 1.25m. Private collection, Daydream Island, Queensland.

Page 99. More Tropical Fish, 1988, 2m x 1.2m. Collection of Jetset Corp. Los Angeles.

Page 158-159. 'They're Racing ', 1984, 5m x 1.5m. Champagne Bar, The Rosehill Racecourse.

Page 167. 'Mad Dogs and...' , 1987, 1.5m x 1.2m. Private collection.

Page 168-169. Pelican Beach, 1984, 2m x 1.1m. Collection, Jetset Ltd., London.

Page 170. Detail from orang utan screen (p. 72).

Page 171. Biggles the Biting Cat, 1984, 1.2m x 1m. Private collection.

Page 173. McCracken & Company, 1988, 5m x 4m. Installation, 500 Collins Street, Ltd., Melbourne.

Page 174-175. Peak Hour, 1986, 4m x 1.4m. Installation, MEPC Australia.

Page 176. From Kirribilli, 1984, 1.8m x 0.5m. Private collection, Sydney.

Page 177. Sydney Harbour Bridge, 1986, 1m x 75cm. Private collection, Sydney.

Page 178-179. Fitzroy Gardens, 1986, 4m x 2m. Installation, The Hilton Hotel, Melbourne.

Page 180. Family Album, 1993, 45cm x 50cm. Exhibition piece.

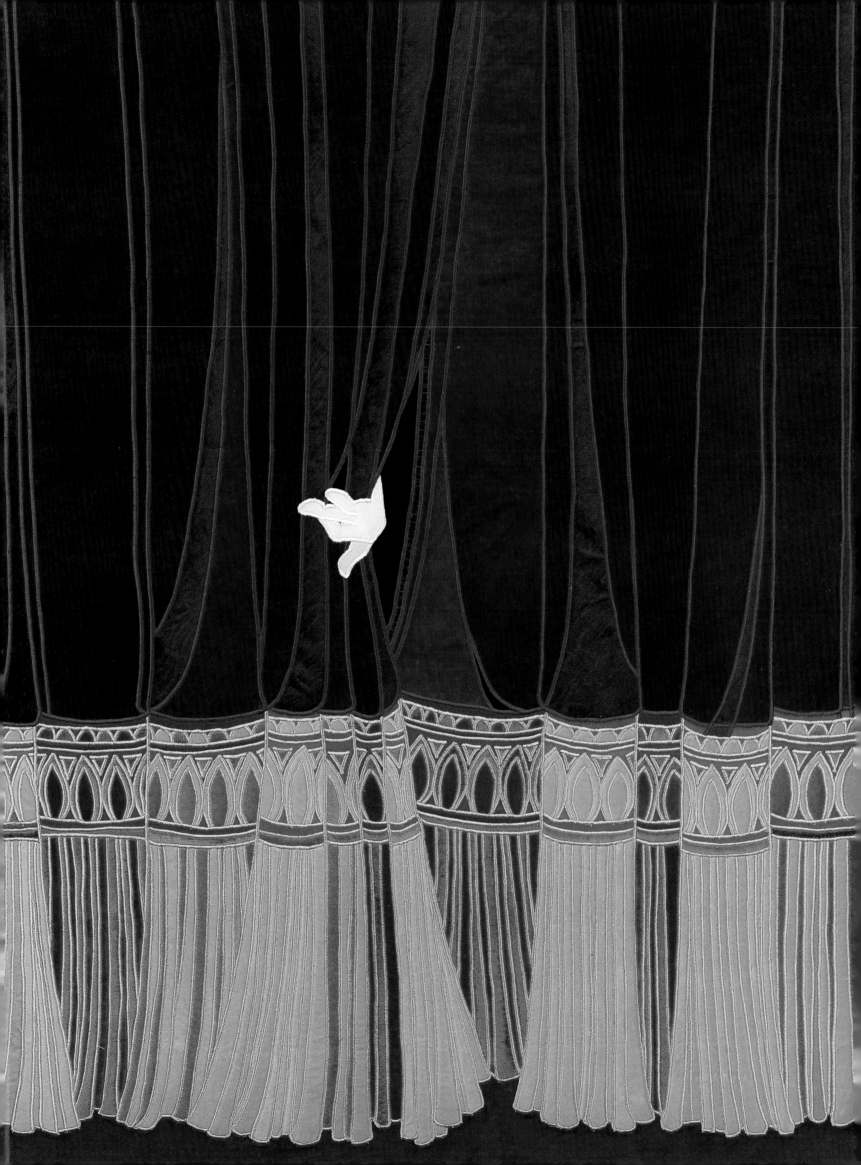